Beginning to

6. 99

Mason and Stephani dd

Bright Ideas
FOR Early Years

Published by Scholastic Ltd
Villiers House, Clarendon Avenue,
Leamington Spa, Warwickshire CV32 5PR

© 1994 Scholastic Ltd
Reprinted 1995

Text © 1994 Hilary Mason and
Stephanie Mudd

Edited by Noel Pritchard
Assistant Editor Kate Banham
Designer Tracey Ramsey
Illustrations by Roger Fereday
Photographs by Martin Soukias
Grateful thanks to the staff and pupils of Park
Hill Primary School, Coventry, who are
featured in these photographs.

Cover design by Anna Oliwa
Cover photograph by Martyn Chillmaid
Waistcoat courtesy of Bonita, Leamington Spa
Artwork by Steve Williams & Associates,
Leicester
Typeset by Typesetters (Birmingham) Ltd
Printed at Alden Press Ltd, Oxford and
Northampton, Great Britain

British Library Cataloguing in Publication Data
A catalogue record for this book is available from the
British Library

ISBN 0-590-53140-9

The right of Hilary Mason and Stephanie Mudd to be
identified as the Authors of this work has been asserted
by them in accordance with the Copyright, Designs and
Patents Act 1988.

Contents

Introduction

This book provides a bank of activities to support you in developing young children as independent and confident writers. Although it is all about writing, you will, in practice, be introducing these skills alongside the other aspects of English, namely, reading, speaking and listening.

Broadly speaking, writing consists of two distinct but interrelated elements — the 'compositional' and the 'secretarial'. The compositional is about creating ideas and translating them into a form that others can follow. It is essential to foster in early years children an ability to think out and talk through stories, sequences and descriptions. Secretarial skills involve the conventions of written language — handwriting, spelling and punctuation. These skills are best taught in context as the children begin to see the need for them.

Young children may not have made the connection between print and the meaning it conveys, but when they first come to you, they already know something about writing. Most of them have encountered signs in the environment and it is highly likely they will also have seen members of their families sending greetings cards or letters, reading newspapers and magazines or writing lists. The activities in this book suggest ways of valuing what the individual child knows and how to build on it. Their own names, for example, infused as they are with personal meaning and interest, can be a powerful way into early writing activities.

One of the most potent factors in children learning to write is the model you (and other adults) provide for them. They see you writing numerous times a day — filling in the register, writing labels, sending messages, writing home to parents. Share this writing with the children so they can see *why* as well as *how* we write. Show them that you too enjoy writing, that you sometimes make mistakes when you just want to get something important down in a hurry, and that this isn't a crime!

Chapter One offers some ideas for setting up a stimulating and supportive writing environment in which to help

even the youngest children feel like the real authors they actually are. Chapter Eight, 'Writing real books', builds on this sense of authorship.

Effective writing will only happen if the children see a real purpose for doing it and understand that we write to convey information or ideas to other people. Chapter Four, 'Stuck for an audience?' highlights the central importance of developing a sense of audience for writing. In Chapter Six, 'Writing across the curriculum', we have given some ideas for looking at writing within maths and science investigations, humanities topics, art and craft, movement and music.

Chapter Five puts the emphasis on 'playing with words', as one of the most effective ways of introducing young children to poetry and rhyme. Chapter Seven, 'Searching for words', provides activities and games which support children as they begin to want to find and write words for themselves.

Children learn to write by being actively involved with writing itself. The most effective way of achieving this is to provide a wide range of opportunities in which they can use and enjoy their writing. This book provides ideas for focusing on the writing element in activities you will already be doing with the children. Aspects of writing can arise naturally from role-play, sharing stories, rhymes and music on the carpet, or going out on a walk around your neighbourhood. In this way children will begin to understand what writing is all about, see the need for it in particular situations and want to write for themselves.

The work of the National Writing Project has had a major impact on approaches to the teaching of writing. They have produced several helpful publications (Thomas Nelson).

Getting started

Chapter one

This chapter suggests ways of setting up a stimulating and supportive environment in which the children can try writing for themselves, without worrying about 'getting it right'.

Immerse the children in writing from the very start and provide them with good writing role models to emulate. Make displaying, discussing and trying out different sorts of writing a part of the children's everyday experiences. Help them to see that writing is about conveying meaning and is fun. Value all their efforts by displaying their writing alongside the work of published authors and encouraging them to share what they have written with others.

Writing corner

Focus
Setting up a stimulating writing environment.

What you need
A wide range of lively 'real writing' for the children to enjoy and use as a model for their own writing: picture and information books, cartoons, greetings cards and postcards, knitting patterns, music manuscripts, poetry, packaging and so on; ball-point and felt-tipped pens, pencils; occasionally ink pens, small brushes, wax crayons and charcoal; different sorts of paper and little books in interesting shapes and colours to tempt the children to write; large sheets of paper for floor work or wall displays; carbon sheets, rubber stamps and ink pads; a typewriter or word processor if possible.

What to do
Try to make the writing area as attractive and inviting as possible. This gives the children important messages about the value of writing. If space is short you could put some materials into a writing box. Share and talk about some of the written material you have selected — what is the writing about and who is it for? Identify various languages and scripts, and discuss the different sorts of print and graphics used.

Immerse the children in writing from the start. Give them plenty of opportunities to write and rewrite in a range of forms based on the writing models on display around them — poetry, stories, notes, lists, letters and cards. Value all their contributions by having a special 'Look at our writing' display board. Invite the children to read some of their writing to other children (or offer to read it with them during carpet time) and encourage them to illustrate their writing to give the readers added enjoyment.

Get the children into the habit of signing their names on anything they write so that others will know who the author is. Foster a sense of independence and enjoyment by giving the children choices about what they write. Encourage them to express their thoughts and ideas without worrying unduly about the technical details. They will see the need to develop writing conventions such as handwriting, spelling and punctuation as they become increasingly enthusiastic and confident about sharing their writing with others.

Look at our names

Focus
Awareness of initial letters in names;
making an alphabet frieze.

What you need
Large, cut-out letters, collage materials,
adhesive, large sheets of paper.

What to do
The letter string in the child's own name is
amongst the first to be recognised by a
young writer. Names are also of great
personal interest, so they provide a
natural launch pad for children's own first
attempts at writing. Making an
alphabetical wall frieze of the children's
names will give them a resource to use
when they want to write messages and
letters to other members of the group.

Encourage the children to 'collage'
each of the letters of the alphabet by
sticking pasta, lentils or fabric on to large
cut-out letter shapes then stick each letter
on to a large piece of paper. Using
textures in this way, and inviting the
children to explore the feel of letters will
help to fix letter configurations in their
minds. Can they trace the letter shapes in
the air?

Show the children how to put the
letters into alphabetical order and ask
them to help you sort out whose names
should be displayed under each initial
letter. Give them some name cards to sort
first, then ask questions such as: 'Where
should we write Carl's name?', 'Does
anybody else's name begin with the
same letter?', 'How do I write the first
letter of Emlyn's name?' Point out that
everybody's name begins with a capital
letter. Help the children to write their own
names and draw a small portrait to place
under their initial letter.

Follow-up
Ask the children for their suggestions
about who else's name they could use to
fill in any gaps you may have on the
frieze. Do any of their parents' or siblings'
names begin with a Y for example? Talk
about where else we come across names,
such as on television, in books and
comics and on packaging. You could add
some of these favourite names to your
frieze.

At home with writing

Focus
Recognising and using different forms of writing found in the home.

What you need
Your play house or play area set up as a living room. Include some examples of the sort of writing (both commercial print and handwritten material) the children are likely to have seen in their living rooms at home: a message pad by the telephone, a letter, catalogues, books, a calendar, newspapers; a range of writing tools (felt-tipped pens, pencils, big crayons and so on).

Preparation
Tell the children they are going to make the play house into a living room. Show them the written material you have selected to put in the play house, and discuss what each item tells us. Ask the children what other kinds of print they have at home, and the sorts of things they have written for themselves or seen others write (sending a birthday card, writing a message for another member of the family, filling in a crossword and so on).

What to do
Let the children play freely in the home corner. Help them to see the need to write things down by asking questions about the domestic situations they are acting out. For example, if they are talking on the telephone, ask 'How will you remember that important message for your mum?' Or, if they are planning to invite some friends over for tea, will they need to make a shopping list or order extra milk?

Encourage the children to bring in more examples of 'home writing' to use in their role play. These may include knitting patterns, postcards, forms and address books.

Watch me write

Focus
Providing a role model for the children's own writing.

What you need
Card for display labels, writing equipment.

Preparation
During the course of your normal working day, there are many occasions when writing is necessary — filling in the register, sending a message to another teacher, writing to parents. Focus the children's attention on this from time to time to help them see the link between why we write and the range of different forms this can take.

What to do
Instead of setting up and labelling a display table after school, for example, make a point of involving the children occasionally. This provides opportunities to introduce beginner-writers to many of the skills and processes they will need in their own writing. As you write the labels, point out the difference between single word labels, such as 'conkers', and those which use more than one word in a phrase, such as 'Pooja brought in all these conkers'. Talk about the importance of leaving spaces between the letters and words. Help the children make the link between the marks on the paper and the messages they give us.

Demonstrate how speech changes when we write it down so that 'under the tree', becomes 'We found these conkers under the chestnut tree'.

Give the children time to watch closely as you talk them through the correct starting positions and consistent letter formation, using helpful words like 'up', 'down', 'round and round', 'tails', 'left' and 'right'.

Follow-up
Ask the children to bring in something to add to a particular display and a label or caption they have written with an adult at home. Alternativley, they might just bring in something to display and you could write the label together.

Write and play

Focus
Setting up opportunities for children to write during their play.

What you need
Story-books and a range of small props to collect together into shoeboxes.

Preparation
The aim is to provide the children with a few simple props and examples of writing which they can incorporate into their play activities. You could, for example, choose to construct a 'party box'. This might include one or two children's picture books, such as *Alfie Gives a Hand* by Shirley Hughes (Picture Lions) or *Spot's Birthday Party* by Eric Hill (Heinemann), a simple party recipe book, an invitation and some blank cards for children to make their own invitations, little cards for labelling the sandwiches, party hats and a thank-you notelet.

What to do
Look at, and talk about, the content of the party box with the children. What are the different sorts of writing for? How could we use them to help us tell a story? Do the children think they need more, or different kinds of labels?

Give them lots of opportunities to use the boxes in their role play when modelling and creating stories with construction toys or Plasticine. Let them build up their own scenarios, using the books for ideas about what to act out. Set challenges to help focus on writing. For example, you could ask them how the guests will know where to sit for tea, or what is in the sandwiches.

Follow-up
Try the same approach with a 'building site' box. You could include a copy of *Big Concrete Lorry* by Shirley Hughes (Walker), or *Miss Brick the Builder's Baby* by J. Ahlberg & C. McNaughton (Viking Kestrel) and equipment such as pieces of wood and toy fencing, tubes, straws for scaffolding, a few stones, order forms to send off for more nails and bricks and a red warning triangle with a 'Wear your hard hat' notice.

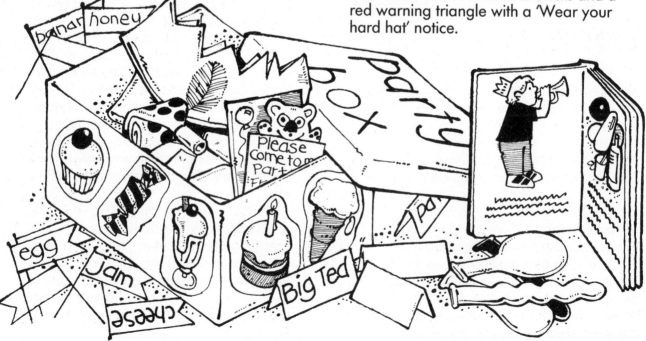

All about books

Focus
Using the book corner as a model for how writing works.

What you need
A selection of children's books and a cosy place to share them.

What to do
You will probably already have a special place where children can sit in comfort to browse through books for pleasure. Make exploring all the different sorts of books (including those with special features such as sound effects, pop-ups and flaps) a regular and enjoyable aspect of your time with the children. Provide some favourite story tapes and show the children how to operate the tape machine to foster a sense of independence. Try using puppets as props to help the children practise their own story-telling techniques. Sharing lots of short, well-structured stories with the children provides them with a model for their own compositional writing. This is also an ideal time for children to match up the storyline to the printed words.

Introduce children to the 'language of books' as you read with them. Always tell them who wrote the book as well as the title — this helps to establish the idea of authorship from the beginning. Point out that in English, we follow the printed words from the front to the back of a book, and from the top of the page to the bottom, tracking from left to right. Gradually, the children will learn to use the same conventions in their own writing.

Your comments please

Focus
Introducing a visitors' book for children to enjoy the written comments of members of the community.

What you need
Sheets of paper folded as a book (or use a scrap book), writing equipment.

What to do
Making a visitors' book is an enjoyable way of providing the children with role models showing other people writing for a real purpose.

Talk to the children about who visits the school — parents, helpers, the nurse, community police officers and so on. Explain that you are going to leave a book out for visitors to sign their names, give the date and write a short comment which you can all enjoy afterwards (see the example below). As visitors come in, ask them to make an entry in the book. Read these with the children regularly. Talk about how we know who has written the message (look under the 'name' heading), and when they came in (under the 'date' heading). Help the children to make the connection between the sorts of comments recorded and the people who wrote them. Some examples might be: 'You crossed the road very nicely today' from the lollipop lady, or 'You shouldn't have any more trouble with that sink now' from the plumber.

Follow-up
Use the same idea, leaving your book out for visitors to fill in, but this time have a theme, such as autumn, toys or journeys. Ask whoever visits you to write something in keeping with your theme.

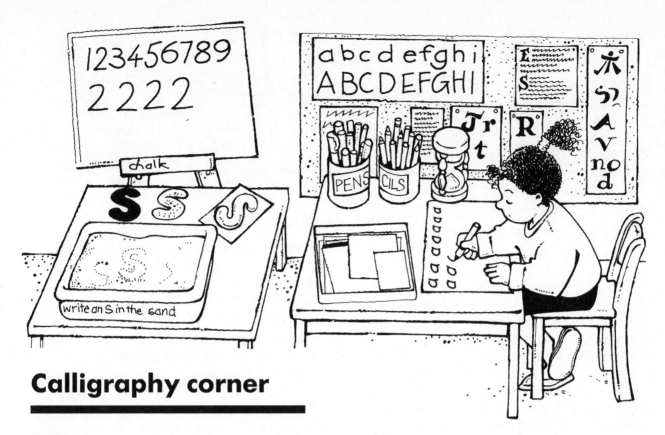

Calligraphy corner

Focus
Developing the skills involved in fluent handwriting.

What you need
A small area of your room or a table set up specially for the children to practise handwriting; pencils, felt-tipped pens, chalk, crayons in various thicknesses, a range of papers in different qualities and colours, Plasticine, a sand or paint tray, interesting displays of handwriting as models for the children (if you are working towards a particular style, you may want to display examples of this more prominently, showing upper and lower case letters); script cards with borders, illuminated letters, examples of complete alphabets and numerals, various scripts (Roman, Chinese and so on). Make sure the writing displayed shows a range of forms including extracts from stories, nursery rhymes, letters, poems and songs.

What to do
The aim is to help the children develop a fluent, relaxed handwriting style where, in their own writing, they can focus on what they want to say without being overly concerned with the formation of each letter. Try to ensure all the children use the calligraphy corner regularly for short activity sessions. Be on hand to check on letter formation, pick up on any potential difficulties individuals may be having and encourage a helpful posture and pencil grip.

Encourage the children to write at a reasonable speed from the beginning. For example, how many As can they write before the sand timer runs out? Teach them letter formation in groups of similar penstrokes, for example, a, b, o and c, to help them get into a flow. Show them where to start individual letters and include a helpful rhyme such as 'all the way round, up and down'.

15

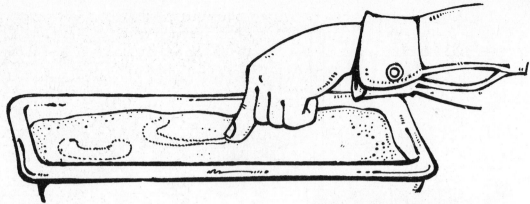

The marks young children make on paper may be largely 'pretend' or 'scribble writing' at first. Channel these into useful handwriting skills by praising any approximations to conventional writing, such as starting at the top of the page, going from left to right in lines across the page, letters started in the right place and so on. Show the children how a particular shape they have made looks just like the 's' for sun on the alphabet frieze. Ask them to 'read back' and talk to you about what they have 'written'. This helps children to make the connection between what they write and what they mean.

Follow-up

• To help develop the movements involved in handwriting patterns, ask the children to use different writing tools to make gentle loops and curves, circular movements, lines and crosses. Use a sand, paint or salt tray to practise anticlockwise and circular movements with forefingers. Encourage them to make pictures using humps, troughs, vertical and horizontal lines.
• Use the photocopiable sheet on page 88 to practise more handwriting patterns. Ask the children to trace over the curtain frill with their forefingers to get the feel of the trough movement. Help them to find the dots for the starting points. Can they find and follow the other trough patterns?

We need a list

Focus
Adult and child writing a list together.

What you need
A parent or adult helper, writing equipment, recipes.

What to do
To help children see that there are good reasons for writing things down, ask an adult you have enlisted to help with cooking activities to prepare a list with the children. They could begin by looking at a recipe together and talking through all the things that go into making the dish. The helper can then suggest that together they write a list to help them remember all the things that have to be bought or collected from home. Depending on the age and ability of the children, their writing may consist of scribble marks next to the adult's conventional writing, pictures, particular letters they recognise from their own names, or some whole words.

The list should then be read through with the children, noting how the words in a list are written under each other from the top to the bottom of the page. Make sure the children see the connection between what they need for their cooking activity and the list they have made.

Writing all around us

Chapter two

Although young children may not have grasped its significance, they are surrounded by print. This chapter suggests activities to help the children see that the writing all around them takes many different forms and tells them many different things. The children's own names are a natural starting-point for writing activities because they have a very personal meaning, and this letter string is among the first to be recognised and used. You will find suggestions for picking up on the writing (including signs and symbols) found in the home, in school and outside in the local environment.

The writing's on me

Focus
Looking at the sorts of words, letters and symbols the children are wearing.

What you need
No special requirements.

What to do
Look at the writing most children will be wearing somewhere on themselves. Identify and talk about slogans on T-shirts and trousers, logos and labels on shoes and boots, care labels in jumpers and coats, letters on soles of shoes and children's own name tags.

Discuss the different styles of lettering and the difference between letters, words and symbols. Ask the children to hunt for the letter 'T' (or another chosen letter) on everybody's clothes — how many letters did they find and where? Can they recognise what these words and letters tell us? Try sorting the words into sets, such as shop names, care labels and personal name labels.

Words and pictures

Focus
Making the distinction between words and pictures.

What you need
Books, newspapers, magazines, catalogues, comics, scissors, three large pieces of paper.

Preparation
Take the time now and again to make sure the children have a clear grasp of the difference between words and pictures. Look at books, magazines, posters and catalogues, helping them to recognise that print has particular characteristics. Ask the children to track, for example, the name 'Anansi' through the text, or spot the frog in the picture you are looking at together. Can they spot letters or whole words (perhaps the name of a product they recognise from advertisements)?

What to do
Give the children the three large sheets of paper and some newspapers, catalogues, comics and magazines to cut up. Ask them to make sets showing pictures, words, both words and pictures. Talk about the different sorts of pictures they have found. Some may be line drawings and charts, for example, while others will be photographs. Can they tell you what the picture is about? What does the writing tell us? Spot the words and pictures on a comic strip.

The name of the game

Focus
Working with the children's names.

What you need
No special requirements.

What to do
Names are one of the first letter patterns recognised and used by those learning to write. Introducing activities and games involving the children's names provides opportunities to highlight writing skills, such as letter configuration, capital letters and spacing. Writing their names also gives the children an early sense of independence.

Encourage the 'signatures habit' from the beginning. Encourage the children to write their names on all completed pieces of work, on their special books, on bar charts, pictograms and on labels to accompany models or precious things brought in from home. Work towards helping the children to write their display labels as a sentence, such as 'Nadia brought in all these stickers'.

Follow-up
● Play some sound games to focus on initial phonics. Ask the children to find a partner whose name begins with the same sound as their own, or call out, for example, 'Darren, Daisy, Amargit' — can the children spot the odd one out? Does anybody else's name begin with that letter?

● To encourage handwriting to 'flow' from the start, give the children one letter from their name (and later letter strings) to practise writing in the sand, salt or paint tray. How many can they write while their partner sings a nursery rhyme?

● Help the children to see that letters combine to make words by asking them to make their names from magnetic or cut-out letters. How many do they need to take from the pile in the middle of the table?

● Help the children to make their initial letters from junk materials, interlocking bricks or using a pegboard. Look carefully at the letter, noting straight and curved lines, sticks and tails.

Hunt the letter

Focus
Developing an awareness of various kinds of print.

What you need
Large plastic, felt or wooden letters; magazines, newspapers, catalogues.

What to do
Give each child an example of the first letter of their name. Help them to get the feel of this letter by tracing round it with them. Demonstrate and discuss how to start in the right place and in which direction to move your hand. What sorts of lines do you have to make – are they all straight or are some curved? Does their letter have any 'tails' or 'sticks?'

With their letters in their hands for reference, can the children find other examples around the room – on posters, charts, displays, in magazines, newspapers and catalogues? Talk about the different sorts of print and typefaces they have noticed. With practice, the children will begin to see the distinctive characteristics of individual letters, irrespective of whether they are handwritten, printed or designed as sophisticated graphics.

Follow-up
The children may enjoy making a personalised letter montage by cutting out their initial letter from magazines, newspapers, cereal packets, catalogues and exploring some of the different fonts available on a printer. Stick these on to a large cut-out outline of the letter shape.

Homing in on writing

Focus
Looking at the different sorts of writing seen and used in the home.

What you need
An example of something you (the teacher) have written for a specific purpose.

Preparation
Show the children an example of something you have written today – this could be a shopping list to remind you what to buy on the way home or an important message you must pass on to another teacher. Ask the children if members of their family have to write things down like that sometimes too. Help them recall the sorts of things they have written at home themselves.

What to do

Use the photocopiable sheet on page 89. Go through the examples of 'home writing' on the sheet with the children and encourage them to tell you about others. The children could take the sheet home and mark the forms of writing they have seen or done this week. Ask them to bring in further examples.

Follow-up

When the children bring in their written examples, talk about where the writing was done, who wrote it and what it was for. Try making a 'matching pairs' display. For example, if somebody has brought in a note to the milkman, this could be displayed next to a milk bottle. Play games with the display, encouraging the children to consider if any of the forms of writing could be matched with different objects.

Notice it!

Focus

Seeing the need for and writing notices for the classroom.

What you need

Card for labels, a poster-sized piece of paper and a marker pen.

What to do

This activity will mean more to the children if it arises naturally from a classroom situation. If, for example, you have been working on a topic about 'How to look after ourselves', the children would see a real purpose for writing a 'Remember to wash your hands please' notice to display in the toilet. Gradually, young writers begin to understand that a message can be left and still mean something when they are not there to say the words themselves.

When you have identified the need for your notice (which may be to keep the painting aprons tidy, or work out how to take turns writing on the computer), talk to the children about the sorts of words you could write. Use labels and notices already in the room to demonstrate that short 'key' words are all you need. As you write, talk through the process. Ask, 'How big will the letters need to be?', 'Do you think I can fit them all on this line?', 'Should I use a capital letter for the first word (or for names)?' Give the children time to match up and say the written words as you point to them.

Ask them for ideas about where the notice should be placed. Establish that it needs to be at their eye level so it can be read easily by all the children.

Writing everywhere

Focus
Exploring the different forms of writing seen in the environment.

What you need
Drawing, painting and writing equipment; card for labels and signs; Blu-Tack or Velcro.

Preparation
Take the children for a walk around your locality and tell them to keep their eyes open for lots of different sorts of writing. Point out the lettering on shops, litter bins, advertising hoardings and street names. Talk about where the writing has been placed — high up, on the sides of buildings or on the pavement. Make sure they understand what the print is telling them.

What to do
Recap on the writing you identified during your walk. Discuss where you saw the different kinds of writing and what it meant. Was it to tell them what time to be at the bus stop or how fast drivers are allowed to go?

Make a wall frieze, at the children's height, of a street scene. Paint or model some shops, a pavement and a road then help the children to print some labels and signs on cards to add to the frieze. Put a piece of Blu-Tack or Velcro on the back of the labels so the children can move them around. Try making signs and labels saying things like: 'Poppies the Florist' on a delivery van, 'litter bin', 'post box', 'Danger, men at work' in a hazard triangle, and a speed restriction sign. Try mixing up the labels — can they put them back in the right place on the frieze?

Shampoo and set

Focus
Recognising and using different types of print found in a hairdresser's.

What you need
Your play area or play house set up as a hairdresser's, writing equipment, magazines or non-fiction books showing different hairstyles.

Preparation
Ask the children to recall and recount their personal experiences of visiting a hairdresser's shop. Can they remember the sorts of writing they saw there? Remind them that shops usually have a name and some signs on the door – can the children remember seeing any of these when they had their hair cut?

What to do
It's a good idea to put some examples of hairdressing-type writing in the play house to get the children started. You could make some of these with the children after your initial brainstorming session – perhaps a message pad by the telephone, an open and closed sign or a price list.

Look at the children's own hairstyles and those shown in books and magazines. Talk about the different possibilities: short 'sculptured' hair, perms, braids, bunches, pony tails, beaded braids and so on.

As the children role play hairdresser and client, help them to see the need for other forms of written information by setting challenges such as 'How will your clients know what time you open and close?', 'How will you know who is coming in today?', 'Have you written their names in the appointment book?', 'How can you tell people not to touch the hot hair dryers?', 'Would your clients like something to read while they wait?'

Here's the secretary

Focus
The opportunity to see an adult writing as part of their job.

What you need
A secretary willing to act as a role model for the children.

Preparation
Make a short visit to the school office to give the children an idea of what happens there. Perhaps you could take the register back together one day, or deliver a note to the secretary. Don't forget to warn the staff in advance!

What to do
Ask the secretary to bring in some examples of the sorts of things she writes during the course of her normal working day. These might include a notebook, some sheets of headed writing paper or a card index showing the children's names and addresses. Encourage the

children to ask questions so that they begin to see the link between the various forms of writing and when the secretary uses them. Perhaps she could show the children their names in her card index and talk about occasions when this might be very useful, such as if children become ill during the day and parents or a doctor need to be contacted. Ask the secretary to leave some samples in the classroom for children to work with later, such as some index cards, forms, name lists and so on.

Follow-up
The children could role play office and secretarial situations, acting out the scribbling down of telephone messages, checking names on dinner or milk lists or filling in an order form for new stationery.

Writing on the outside

Focus
Becoming more aware of print on packaging.

What you need
Empty packets, bottles and boxes.

Preparation
Look at the writing on the outside of your empty boxes, packets and bottles. Make sure the children can discriminate between the words and the pictures. Discuss the different sizes and shapes of lettering.

What to do
Focus the children's attention on the words that tell us what is inside the packet. Look more closely at a particular

container. Establish that it is not the picture of the tiger on the front of the box, or the cut-out dinosaur mask on the back, that tells us what's inside, but the letters that make up the name of the product. Play a game of 'spot the brand name' on cereal boxes, biscuit packets, flour bags and so on.

Can the children sort the containers into sets, such as things we eat and things we use to keep clean? As the children are sorting, encourage them to explain how they know which sets various products belong to. For example, 'I know this is cat food because my cat eats Whiskers' or 'I know it's Frosties because my name starts with that letter.'

Follow-up
Use the containers to set up a shop. Tell the children that they must first make a shopping list to help them remember what to buy and refer them back to the packets as reminders for how to write the words. Praise attempts at all levels – pictures, symbols, scribble writing or correct use of a first letter or letter string.

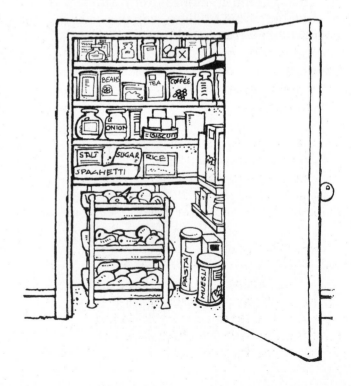

Road signs

Focus
Recognising road signs and using them in structured play.

What you need
A large sheet of paper to make a road play mat, writing equipment, pictures or models of road signs (a copy of *The Highway Code* will be useful).

Preparation
Take the children out to look at road signs. Start from the immediate school environment, spotting the signs in the car park and the zigzag lines outside the school gates. Can the children see a 30m.p.h. road sign nearby?

Draw their attention to all the most obvious information signs, such as the lollipop person's stick, traffic lights, a bridge symbol and so on. Talk about what the signs mean and why they are in certain places rather than others. Who are the signs meant for – drivers or pedestrians – and what information do they give?

What to do
When you are back in class discuss some of the signs you saw outside. Recap on what they were for and where you saw them. Show the children some pictures to remind them what the signs looked like then choose a small number of these to make with the children (crossing patrol sign, speed limit, traffic lights) to use on a play mat. Use a commercial play mat or make a simple mat of your own from a large sheet of paper to represent the road system around the school, as shown in the illustration above.

The choice is yours

Focus
Recognising and using picture symbols.

What you need
Pieces of card, drawing and writing equipment.

Preparation
Can the children recall seeing picture symbols when they've been out and about? Can they remember seeing the picture on the toilet door, the 'no smoking' sign in the school entrance hall, or the pictures on the floor guide in a department store? Have they made the connection between the pictures and the message they convey?

What to do
Introduce the idea of a 'choice table' to the children. Tell them they will be able to choose a certain sort of activity from a picture guide (see the illustration below). Get the children's ideas about the sorts of things they could use on the table top. These might include Plasticine, lacing cards, jigsaws, dominoes or fuzzy felt.

Talk about what kind of picture would best sum up the materials they have suggested — perhaps a lace for lacing cards or a jigsaw piece. Do the children think it's necessary to add all the details, or does this really matter as long as the message is clear? Ask the children to draw their suggested symbols on card. You can then decide before the children come in what you would like them to choose from that day and display the symbols on a chart for them to refer to.

Early ways into writing

Chapter three

Children's early scribble writing represents an essential stage in their development as writers. Through their first efforts, they can find out which marks are important and begin to understand that these marks carry meaning. Whatever the children write, take the time to talk about it with them. Praise both the content (what they are trying to say) and any features of their print that are close to conventional writing.

In order to develop the language of writing young children need opportunities to tell stories. The ability to work out a sequence of events is also important in many forms of writing. Use the 'Breakthrough to Literacy' approach (using word cards to build up sentences on a sentence maker stand) sometimes to help children feel in control of words in these early stages.

Write this way

Focus
Developing left to right orientation for writing.

What you need
A tray containing damp sand, assorted small toys such as Lego people and vehicles.

Preparation
Make the most of any opportunities that arise to discuss the left to right nature of writing. Show the children how this works in books as you read stories together, and point it out as you help the children compose their own words and sentences.

What to do
As the children are playing in the damp sand, encourage them to make up simple scenarios to help them develop left to right orientation. For example, ask them to try taking a toy person to the garage. Show them how to place the person on the left and the garage on the right. Can they make a straight pathway from one to the other? Try taking a dog to the kennel, a bird to a nest or a bus to the bus stop. Keep the pathways straight at first, pointing out that this is the quickest route.

As the children develop their left-right skills further, encourage them to make zig-zag or wavy pathways from one side of the sand tray to the other. Make sure they always start on the left and end on the right. These line patterns are an integral part of handwriting and also help the children's hand movements to 'flow'.

Follow-up
Use the photocopiable sheet on page 90 to reinforce these patterns. Ask the children to draw pathways from left to right for each of the four frames. Ask them to tell the story of where, for example, the bird is going and why. Trace the pathways with index fingers then draw them in. For the bus and the car, can the children keep their lines inside the roadways?

Look and remember

Focus
Making a picture reminder list.

What you need
A flip chart and marker pen, drawing and writing equipment.

Preparation
You can make picture lists of any cumulative song or rhyme such as 'If you're happy and you know it', 'There was an old woman who swallowed a fly', or 'Old MacDonald had a farm'. Make sure the children are familiar with the words.

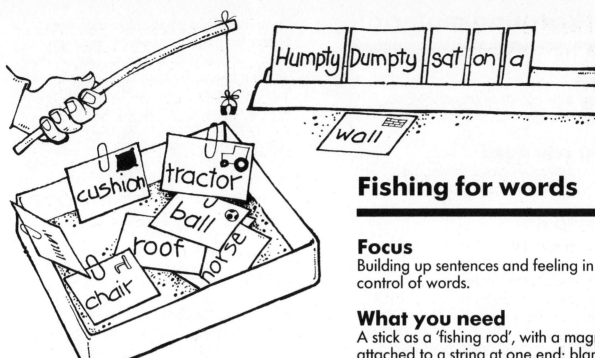

Fishing for words

Focus
Building up sentences and feeling in control of words.

What you need
A stick as a 'fishing rod', with a magnet attached to a string at one end; blank word cards with a paper-clip on one end; a sentence stand.

What to do
On separate pieces of card write the words of the first line of a nursery rhyme (or use a sentence from the children's own writing) and put it in a sentence stand like the one in the illustration. Point to the words as you say them together.

Make up some new sentences based on the original. Ask for ideas about what else Humpty might be sitting on (tractor, roof, castle . . .). Write each of these words on a 'magnetic' card and put the cards into a 'pool'. Play a fishing game to 'catch' one of the word cards and use it to substitute the last word of your original sentence, for example Humpty Dumpty sat on a . . . tractor. Read the sentences back each time.

Try changing Humpty Dumpty for traditional story characters, such as a dragon, princess or giant (The . . . sat on a . . .). In this way the children can generate lots of sentences of their own, see how they are built up and begin to feel in control of their own writing.

What to do
Did the children find the sequence of your chosen song or rhyme difficult to remember? Introduce the idea of a picture list which will remind them of the order in which things happen. Go through each verse of 'Old MacDonald had a farm', for example. Ask the children to tell you which animal the song introduces first then show them how you could draw a little cow at the top of the paper. Ask the children which animal comes next, and establish that the picture symbols should be placed under each other like a list. This helps to reinforce the idea that we usually move through written text from the top to the bottom of a page as shown below. If the children are already comfortable with this convention, you could suggest they use other ordering notations, such as numbers or arrows. Some children might like to try writing the word next to their pictures. Brainstorm other animals to draw and add to the list to make verses of your own.

Background material

Focus
Making a simple story sequence based on a familiar setting.

What you need
Large sheets of paper, drawing and painting materials, simple puppets.

What to do
With your help the children will be making a small wall frieze (at child height) to use as a backdrop for story telling. Choose a setting with which the children are very familiar, such as the local shopping centre, park or adventure playground. Alternatively, you could base the frieze on a visit you have made to the seaside or wildlife park.

Discuss which elements the children want to include on the frieze, such as swings, flower beds, a sand pit, trees and an ice cream stall to make a park scene, for example. Cut these out and stick them on to the frieze paper to make your backdrop as shown in the illustration below. Invite the children to use the frieze and the props to make up some stories to tell their friends. Pick up on what they are saying to help develop a sequence through their stories so that others will be able to follow and enjoy it. Ask questions like 'What are the children on the swings calling out to each other?', 'What is going to happen next — perhaps the puppy runs off with dad's ice cream?', 'What has made the park keeper upset?'

Begin with a limited number of props (stick, finger or box puppets) and help the children to decide which characters these might represent (for example, adults, children and dogs). With practice, the children will be able to add more characters and detail to their stories. Providing the children with opportunities to explore the language of story telling helps them to compose their own written stories.

Get in sequence

Focus
Sequencing events.

What you need
Three sheets of paper for each child in the group, drawing and writing materials.

What to do
The children will be drawing a three-frame sequence describing what happened before and after a main event. This helps them to focus on the need for a structure in their writing, especially the beginning, middle and ending of stories. They will be building this up over time, just as real writers do.

Talk to the children about an event they can remember very clearly, such as a recent celebration or shopping trip, an accident they had, kicking a ball and so on. Ask them to draw a picture of this event on one of the sheets of paper. In the shopping example, the child could draw the middle frame showing themselves going into a shop. Ask, 'What sort of shop is it?', 'Did anyone go with you?' The pictures need not be complex but they should have enough detail to help the children retell their stories later.

At another time, draw the next frame on the second sheet of paper, showing what led up to the previous picture. Ask, 'Why did you go to the shop?' The child may tell you she went to the shoe shop because she had a hole in her wellies and needed a new pair and then draws a picture to sum this up. Subsequently, work with the child to complete the story sequence by drawing a picture of what happened last of all (splashing through puddles in new boots and so on). The three frames can then be used to retell the story.

Follow-up
● Shuffle the sequence and reorder it. Try giving the three frames to friends — do they come up with the same sequence?
● Use the photocopiable sheet on page 91 for further sequence work. Cut each story strip into three frames and stick them on card for the children to put in sequence and tell a story. They may come up with different story versions from the same sequence, which is fine so long as it makes sense when they tell it.

Our favourites

Focus
Writing names as a way of collecting data.

What you need
Empty cereal packets, paper and pencils.

What to do
This activity investigates 'favourite' breakfast cereals. Ask the children to cut out the names from the cereal packets and stick them on separate pieces of paper. Make sure they understand it is the word showing the product name they need to cut out, rather than any of the other print on the packet.

Ask each child to write their names on the sheet of paper showing their favourite kind of cereal. Check to make sure they have understood that by writing their own name under the name of the cereal they are leaving a record of their personal favourite. Discuss your findings. Count the names under each heading to find out which cereal is the most popular. Try the same approach to investigate other favourites, such as snack bars, toys or places to visit.

Holiday time

Focus
Recognising and using different sorts of writing through role play.

What you need
Your play house or a section of the room set up as a travel agent's, some travel brochures and posters, drawing and writing equipment.

Preparation
Talk to the children about what a travel agent does – can they remember visiting one to book a holiday or buy train tickets? Invite those who have travelled abroad to share their experiences. Look at travel brochures and posters advertising exciting locations and help the children to see that the printed material gives us the information we need to help us plan a holiday.

What to do
As the children are role playing customer and travel agent, encourage them to use the brochures and posters to choose where they would like to go. Do they like hot, relaxing holidays, or do they fancy something a bit more energetic, such as skiing or climbing? Praise and build on scenarios where the children practise looking things up in the brochures or on maps, filling in forms, writing a letter or making tickets.

As the children play, they may see the need to use other sorts of writing such as a message pad by the telephone, timetables, maps, booking forms and tickets. They could try making some of these for themselves.

'I can't sleep'

Focus
Using narrative to develop the language of writing.

What you need
A collection of no-text picture books, or stories with very few words.

Preparation
Share a range of minimal/no-text picture books with the children to help them develop their own story-telling skills. *I Can't Sleep* by Philippe Dupasquier (Walker) is an excellent example.

What to do
Tell the children to work in pairs and ask each pair to select a no-text book to retell. Make sure they know what the story is about. Discuss the main sequence of events as portrayed through the pictures. Check that the children are moving through the book from left to right, following the story sequence. Help them to identify the main characters and what their names might be. Can they use different voices to highlight how the characters seem to be feeling?

Discuss the setting of the story – where is it taking place? Talk about how the story starts. What other sorts of story beginnings can they remember that might be useful? What happens at the end? As the children's confidence grows, you could encourage them to add more detail – just as you would with written stories. Look more closely at some of the pictures – what clues can they spot to help predict what might happen next? Do the characters look happy, excited, tired?

The children might like to think of a refrain to use at certain key points in the story, such as 'What is it now?' or 'Please go to sleep.'

Just like mine

Focus
Encouraging the use of detail and more precise language.

What you need
Farm sets which feature identical sets of fencing, animal housing and pairs of animals.

What to do
Tell the children to work in pairs. Give each child a small set of farm toys — make sure they both have the same number and type of pieces. The children should sit on either side of a screen or chalkboard so they can hear, but not see each other. Child A makes a simple farm layout, and child B has to replicate it by listening carefully to his partner's instructions. For example, child A could have two fields with three sheep in one and two cows in another. Compare the two layouts — how similar are they? Can the children think of reasons for any differences? As they become more proficient at this, encourage them to make more complicated layouts and give their partners more detail. Encourage the children to ask questions like 'Are the cows standing up or lying down?', 'Have you used the mummy cow or the baby one?', 'Are they black or white sheep?'

Playing this sort of 'copy cat' game provides opportunities for children to practise using more detail and descriptive language, which lays the foundations for their own writing.

All change!

Focus
The importance of word order in sentences.

What you need
Strips of card long enough for a sentence containing four to six words, a piece of paper folded in half like a book.

What to do
This activity works best if the sentences you choose come from the children's own writing or from an activity in which you are currently engaged.

Make up some simple sentences with the children such as 'Dad sat on the chair.' Write this sentence on a strip of card, saying each word as you write it, and read the finished sentence through together. Draw attention to the spaces you have left between th[...] the child to cut the sente[...] separate words then ju[...] work together to reco[...] sentence. Talk about [...] wrote first and ask, '[...] Read the sentence aga[...] draw a picture of this sentenc[...] left-hand side of the folded page.

At another time, take the same sentence and shuffle the words. Play with, and say, the words as you arrange them in different ways. Which ones make sense and which are gobbledegook? Decide on a sentence, such as 'The chair sat on dad.' Draw a picture of this on the opposite side of the folded page. Give the children the two sets of words to put in a little folded paper pocket at the bottom of the page as shown in the illustration. You could compile some of these into a class book and invite each child to read their own double-page spread to others.

done!

Focus
Understanding that writing is meant to be read; recognising the need for writing 'conventions'.

What you need
No special requirements.

What to do
Tell the children they are going to make a book all about what they like doing best in class. Ask them to draw a simple picture of their favourite activity and write a sentence about it underneath (at whatever level they can manage). As you discuss the pictures and writing with individual children, respond positively to their efforts. Praise them for any helpful elements that indicate they are beginning to see a connection between the marks they have made and the meaning they are trying to convey. Congratulate them for any recognisable letter shapes or words, and for writing across the page from left to right. Perhaps they have used one of the letters in their name or made a squiggle that closely resembles a letter you wrote for them earlier.

Without devaluing the children's attempts, help them to see the need for conventional recording so that the words can still be read when they are not actually there to say them. Suggest that it might be a good idea, just to make it really clear, if you wrote the sentence too. Show them how you form the letters and put the words in a certain order so that others can follow them easily. Include the children's sentences alongside your own transcriptions in the book so that they have a model to refer to.

Follow-up
Invite parents to write about what they liked doing best when they were at school to add to the class book.

IT and me

Focus
Using the children's names to introduce them to a computer keyboard.

What you need
A computer with a software program offering a range of fonts, a printer.

What to do
Help the children to find their way round the keyboard by asking them to type in their own names. Show them how to use the shift key to write the capital letters at the beginning of their names. Ask them to look at the screen and say the names of the letters they have keyed in.

The children can then enjoy printing out their names in different types of lettering — enlarged, italics, gothic, copperplate and so on. This will not only help them to learn the special letter string that makes up their own names, but also clues them into recognising that the writing all around them can be written in all sorts of different typefaces.

Stuck for an audience?

Chapter four

All writers need an audience. This chapter highlights the need for children to see that we write so that other people can share our thoughts, feelings, ideas and knowledge. This in turn helps them to see the reason why there are certain basic writing conventions, such as spelling, punctuation and handwriting. Encourage the children to behave like real writers from the beginning. Help them to identify who a particular piece of writing is for and the best way of getting the message across. Try to develop the habit of writing their names on all pieces of writing so that other people will know who the author is.

Love from . . .

Focus
Looking at how letters are set out and the concept of corresponding regularly.

What you need
A 'post-box' made from a carton with a cut-out letter slot, some examples of letters sent to the school office, *Frog and Toad Are Friends* by Arnold Lobel (Young Puffin).

Preparation
Read the children the Frog and Toad story. Discuss why we write letters to our friends. Show the children some school mail, and note that the envelopes all show the school address on the front.

What to do
Have a closer look at the Frog and Toad letter (or any other sample letter you choose). How does the letter begin? Establish that the opening written convention for letters is 'Dear . . .'. Write this for the children to help fix it in their minds. Frog ended his letter by writing 'Your best friend, Frog'. Do the children know what else we write at the end of letters? Focus on one ending such as 'love from' and demonstrate how this is written.

Invite the children to write to their friends regularly. They can write anything they choose or simply send a drawing. Tell them that they must start with 'Dear . . .' and sign their name at the end. Make sure the envelope (or the outside of the folded paper) is clearly marked with the name of the receiver. Let them post their letters in the class post-box and take turns to play postman. Write to the children yourself sometimes.

Follow-up
Extend your internal postal system to the wider school audience, perhaps suggesting that a post-box becomes a fixture in the school entrance hall. Siblings, friends, teaching staff, helpers and parents can then correspond with each other too.

Scrumptious suggestions

Focus
Making picture menus to suggest favourite meals to the cook.

What you need
Card, old magazines, scissors, writing and drawing equipment.

Preparation

Talk to the children about their favourite foods — what would they most like for lunch? Which school meals or packed lunches do they enjoy best?

What to do

Tell the children they are going to suggest some favourite meals the cook might make for them. They then each choose their favourite meal and draw or cut out pictures to stick on card. Talk to the children about making sure the menu is clear and easy to follow. Are the pictures self-explanatory or would it be a good idea to include captions or labels showing various parts of the meal? The menus could then be collected into a suggestion box for the cook to use.

Follow-up

• The cook could make some of these meals for real sometimes, displaying the picture menu and a 'Thank you' to the person who suggested it.
• Children who have snacks or packed lunches could make some picture menu suggestions in the same way to take home to their parents.

You'll like this one

Focus

Recommending books to help others with their choice of reading material.

What you need

The children's favourite stories, paper, pencils and crayons.

What to do

When you bring the children together for story time, invite them to choose one of their favourite stories for you to read with

them again. You could go on to make a special display of these books.

Ask the children who else they think might like to read some of these books. Discuss how they could get their ideas across to other people when they are not there to enthuse about them face-to-face. Suggest that they draw a picture about a favourite book they would like to recommend to other people. Make sure they write their names under the picture so others will know who is recommending it. Older children could also write the title and author on their pictures.

Follow-up

• Involve parents in these early stages of book reviewing. When a child takes home a favourite book, ask parents to write down what their children said about it. The children could then bring these reviews into class and display them alongside their pictures. Encourage parents to use the children's book reviews to help them choose what to borrow from the library or buy from the bookshop.
• You could give the children a wider audience for their 'good books' suggestions by sending them to the public library for display.

Look what we've done

Focus
Giving a clear message to an identified audience.

What you need
Any work in progress, card for labels, writing equipment.

What to do
As the children are working, stop occasionally and ask them who else they think might like to see some of the things they have made or written. Sometimes they will feel that they have written something just for themselves. This is fine, but at other times they may like to share their writing with parents, other children or members of the local community.

Consider where their work could be displayed so that other people can enjoy it too. Does anything need a label to provide extra information when the children are not there to talk about it themselves? Have they written their names on their work so others will know who has done it?

Discuss how to make sure that fragile models can be kept safely. Where would be a good place to put them? What sign could be left next to them to keep them safe? Encourage them to see the need sometimes to leave the caretaker a note saying something like 'Sorry about the mess, I need this tomorrow. From Suhayl'.

Seed sequence

Focus
Recording an activity as a sequence for others to follow.

What you need
Seeds, a plant pot, potting compost, a watering can, cut-out paper arrows.

Preparation
Work with individuals or a small group to plant some seeds. Focus the children's attention on the order in which they must do things to plant the seed correctly. As you are planting, go through the sequence using words like 'First you need to . . ., then you . . . Next we take . . . Finally it goes in the pot ready to grow.'

What to do
Talk the children through the sequence once more to recap on the order in which you did things. Ask them to share what they now know about seed planting with their friends by making a display from the real objects used.

Can the children show the sequence by setting out the objects used in order and linking the stages with paper arrows? Help them to make the connection between being able to move the objects around until the sequence is correct and how we can order or change words when we write.

Follow-up

When the children are satisfied their sequence is displayed in the correct order, encourage them to talk it through with their friends as a 'report back' session. They might decide that it would be a good idea to add some picture or word captions to make the sequence even easier to follow.

Notice-board

Focus

Setting up a class notice-board and recognising a wide range of writing.

What you need

Space for a display board at a level suitable for children to use, paper, writing and drawing equipment.

Preparation

Talk with the children about the sorts of things they have seen on notice-boards. If you have one in the room discuss the sorts of notices and messages written on it. Who is the writing intended for? What's special about this kind of writing? Tell the children you are going to clear the board and start again so that you can all leave messages for each other.

What to do

Set the example yourself by writing a message to the whole class, such as; 'Don't forget your wellies on Friday.' You could add a picture to make your message more accessible to the youngest children. Talk about why you decided to use the notice-board to communicate with them today. Establish that it is a good way to reach lots of people simultaneously and saves you having to write out the same words 30 times!

Ask the children if there are any notes, reminders or messages they would like to put up on the notice-board. Use it regularly yourself and encourage the children to add writing, invitations and drawings done at home. Accept all contributions, the only proviso being that their name must be on it.

Follow-up

When the notice-board begins to look cluttered, decide with the children how you could make it more ordered. Perhaps you could divide it into sections with headings such as 'Lost and Found', 'Advertisements' and 'Parents' corner'.

I am a princess. Kim

You need
hat
shawl
boots
Dress like a giant

Jan

All dressed up

Focus
Compiling an ideas book to help children understand how and why we communicate ideas in writing.

What you need
A collection of dressing-up clothes, including shawls, drapes, lengths of soft fabric and so on, for the children to put on in the play house.

What to do
As they dress up as various characters and act out different scenarios, talk to individual children about their interesting – or outlandish – 'costume'. Ask them to tell you what they are wearing and who they have become. Praise their inventiveness and suggest they might like to find a way of sharing their ideas with others by contributing to a book.

The children could begin by making a careful drawing of each item used in the 'dressing-up kit'. Some of the children can try to write explanatory labels and captions such as 'a long veil', 'wellie boots' or 'This is Jane dressed up as a bride'. Compile these individual contributions in a 'Who do you want to be?' book to leave by the play house for role play ideas.

Who's who

Focus
Giving information about school helpers to a wider audience.

What you need
Writing and drawing materials.

Preparation
Talk about who works in the school and the sorts of jobs they do. Try making a checklist with the children of teachers, helpers and so on. Can they describe what some of these people look like? Discuss how you could let new children or visitors know about these people.

What to do
Ask the children to paint a portrait or make a collage picture of some key school personnel: teachers, secretary, nurse, cook, caretaker. Encourage the children to think about what else the portraits might need to make the message clearer. Compose a sentence to accompany each portrait. Talk through which words the children would like to use and how to get the message across clearly. For example, a child might say: 'It's Ms Broomly.' Show how speech can change when we write it: 'This is Ms Broomly.' Then ask 'Have we told people what Ms Broomly does?' Encourage the children to develop captions that read something like: 'This is Ms Broomly. She cleans the school for us.' Read the caption through and consider whether everyone will be able to understand what has been written. You could scribe for some children while others will be able to try writing the words for themselves.

Now that you have your 'rogues gallery' ask for the children's ideas about the best place to display it so that as many people as possible will be able to share the information.

Follow-up
Once the pictures are pinned up in the entrance hall (or some other prominent position), ask the adults to add a short piece of writing about themselves under their own portraits. It would be ideal if the children could watch as they write.

This is Ms Broomly. She cleans the school for us.

Poster power

Focus
Making an information poster to display in the local community.

What you need
Some examples of posters the children are likely to have seen in health centres, dental surgeries or specialist shops; paper, magazines.

Preparation
This activity will work best if the subject of the poster arises naturally from a current topic. Look at some posters together and talk about what is special about them. How is the message put across? What do the letters and words tell us? How big are they? Are there pictures to give us further information?

Recap on what the children already know about keeping their teeth healthy. Decide on a suitable caption for your poster and write it down so everyone can see it. You may choose something like 'Have you brushed your teeth today?' or 'These foods are good for you.' Consider how big the lettering needs to be. How should the words be arranged so they all fit on the poster and are easy to read? The children can draw round or cut out letters to arrange on the paper. They could then draw or cut out magazine pictures of foods, tooth brushes and so on and combine them with the lettering to make an eye-catching poster with a strong message.

What to do
You may have been finding out how to look after teeth as part of a topic on 'Ourselves' or 'Food'. Tell the children they will be making some posters to put up in a dental surgery so that others can share what they know.

Follow-up
Try the same approach for posters to put up in the library ('Have you read the new book by Margaret Mahy?'), at the swimming baths ('Please use the footbath') or at the police station ('Wear something white at night').

Invitations

Focus
Writing invitations and deciding who to send them to.

What you need
Some examples of party invitations, card or good quality paper of suitable size to make your own.

Preparation
Build on times when you and the children might naturally want to have a party — perhaps at the end of a 'Celebrations' topic, or to say thank you to helpers and friends. Show the children some invitations and talk about the sorts of words and conventions used on them. What is the essential information we want to get across?

What to do
With the children work out a format for your invitation. Show them how to write headings such as 'Please come to my party on', 'Time' and 'Place'. Write these headings in one colour as a list and decide with the children what to write in the appropriate spaces. Who is the invitation to? Have they told their guests who the invitation is from? Use a different colour for the words which accompany the headings.

Once you have composed your invitations ask the children to help you make a list of people they would like to invite to their party — helpers, senior citizens to repay them for a visit last term, the vicar and so on.

Follow-up
Use the invitation on the photocopiable sheet on page 92 to familiarise the children with the invitation format. Later they may want to design their own.

Can we help?

Focus
Making an information chart to help share information and skills.

What you need
No special requirements.

What to do
Pick up on something you notice individual children doing well; perhaps a skill like tying shoelaces, or the ability to use more than one language. You could use carpet times to focus on particular things individuals know about, such as countries they have visited, going to the dentist or a new pet.

Suggest to the children that it might be a good idea to share knowledge with others who may not have our 'expertise'. Ask the children to draw and caption one thing they feel they are good at and could help others with. Compile these into a picture information chart like the one shown.

When the children ask you for help, refer them to your 'experts list' from time to time to see if another child could help them instead. Add to your list as new skills emerge and knowledge grows. Invite parents or helpers to add their names to your list of 'experts'.

Writing on the ward

Focus
An opportunity to meet and use different forms of writing in hospital role play.

What you need
Your play house or play area set up as a hospital; any simple props you have such as nurses' uniforms or a doctor's bag; non-fiction books, paper, pencils.

Preparation
Tell the children you are going to set up a hospital in the play house and that they are going to think about the sorts of writing staff and patients need to do. Share personal experiences of hospitals — do the children know anybody who works in one? Have they ever had to stay in hospital themselves, or visited relatives or friends there?

What to do
Let the children make up their own scenarios and play freely in their new hospital environment. Provide some particular forms of writing such as message pads and temperature charts to start them off. As the children are playing ask them questions like 'How can the nurse make sure the patients get the right medicines?', 'Do we need to leave a message for the doctor to read next time she does her ward round?', 'Would the patient like some notelets by the bed in case he feels like writing to Grandma or friends?'

Direct a duck

Focus
Using a programmable toy to make a set of instructions for others to follow.

What you need
A Roamer, Valiant Turtle or equivalent (which the children know how to use), a set of instruction cards, a farmyard set.

What to do
Set up a simple farmyard scene (as shown below). Can the children direct the 'duck' (programmable toy) from the fence to the pond? Give them some cards on which you have written the key words 'forwards', 'backwards', 'left' and 'right'. Talk the sequence through with the children as they try out how many units to move. Write the number of units on the cards as you go along, altering commands as necessary. You should end up with a sequence of commands to take the duck successfully back to its pond.

Try out the command sequence. Can a friend direct the duck using the sequence? Do you need to change the order or number of units? Older children could try writing their own sequence cards, or write abbreviations such as F4 or L2.

Follow-up
Ask the children to write a sequence to show others how to use a tape recorder or computer. Could a friend follow their instructions easily? Do any of the instructions need clarifying?

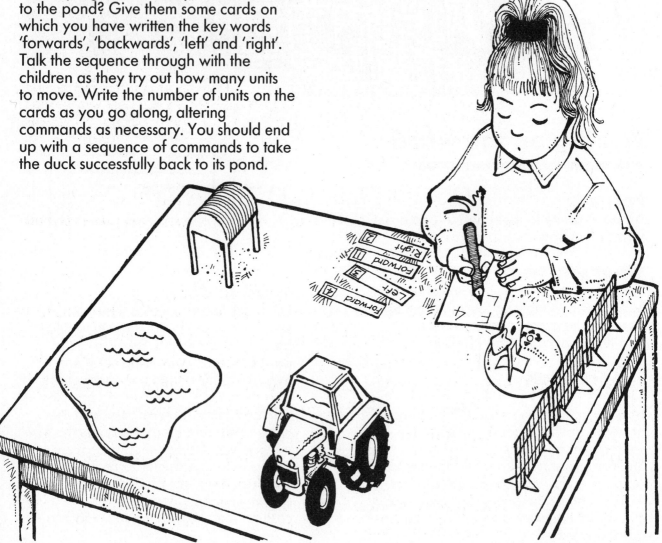

Playing with words

Chapter five

Beginner writers need to feel at ease with words if they are to enjoy writing. Words can be funny, interesting, nonsensical, sometimes beautiful. Putting the accent on responding to, and getting involved in, aspects of poetry and rhyme helps the children feel in control of our complex language.

Play lots of oral games with the children and immerse them in rhymes to help them enjoy the sounds and rhythms of words. Make poetry and rhyme part of the children's structured play. Give them opportunities to 'feel' words through body movement and music.

We know all these

Focus

Making a list of rhymes the children know and can share.

What you need

Writing and drawing equipment, a chalkboard or flip chart and marker pens.

Preparation

Give the children lots of opportunities to tell, sing and play rhymes and poems to help them recognise these as a special form of writing. To provide the children with good role models, you could set up a simple display of poetry books and stories which use rhyme as an integral part of the text.

What to do

You are going to be making a list with the children of all the rhymes they know and can say. Start by showing them how to write the title of a rhyme you have sung or acted out recently. Discuss how you could make a little picture symbol next to the title, as an extra clue to help them remember the rhyme.

How many more rhymes do the children know? Add these to the list. Can they teach a favourite rhyme to other children in the group? Write out these titles or first lines and add more as the children learn them. Pin the list up at a height suitable for the children so they can refer to it during their own writing activities.

Follow-up

● You could use the list as a starting point for an anthology. The children each choose one of the titles on the list and then illustrate the rhyme on a separate page. You or another adult can help the children to write out the words of the rhymes next to their pictures. The rhymes can then be collected into a loose-leaf folder.
● Record the rhymes on tape so the children can use the anthology to match up the words as they sing along. Invite parents in to teach the children some of the rhymes they know to add to your collection.

Rhymes we know

1. Old King Cole
2. Hickory, Dickory Dock
3. Jack and Jill
4. Little Miss Muffet
5. Twinkle twinkle little star

Poetry in motion

Focus
Responding to poems through movement; developing a sense of audience.

What you need
Play Rhymes by Marc Brown (Picture Lions).

What to do
Teach the children the traditional action rhyme 'Teddy bear, teddy bear turn around. Teddy bear, teddy bear touch the ground.' Say it together emphasising the strong rhythmic pattern. For added enjoyment and to help the children understand the meaning of the poem, ask them to think of, and try out some appropriate actions to accompany the words. These might include spinning round, bending down to touch the floor or putting hands together.

Divide the children into two groups, one to be the performers and the other to be the audience. Encourage the 'performers' to use a range of voices for different action lines (big, strong voices for 'Teddy bear, teddy bear that will do', or quiet voices for 'say goodnight'). You could practise starting off with big voices, getting gradually softer as teddy goes to bed. Sharing poems and rhymes in this way not only helps to make the meaning of the words clearer, but also highlights the central importance in writing of conveying our message clearly to other people.

Follow-up
Ask the children to listen carefully while you read them a poem with a strong atmosphere such as a lullaby. Tell them you would like them to think about how the sounds of the words make them feel. As you read it again, ask the children to practise some appropriate body movements to go with it. These could be rocking slowly from side to side, making cradling and swaying movements with their arms or large floating and swirling movements around the room.

Try a contrasting poem such as one about a machine or stormy weather.

Sally go round the sun

Focus
Adapting a well-known rhyme as a way into writing poetry.

What you need
No special requirements.

What to do
One of the easiest ways of introducing children to the skills involved in selecting words and writing poetry is to adapt a well-known rhyme.

Teach the children the following verse:

Sally go round the sun,
Sally go round the moon,
Sally go round the chimney pots
On a Saturday afternoon.

Have fun saying or singing it until the children know the words really well. Ask them to clap every time they say, or hear you say, the word 'Sally'. This will clue them in to which word you are going to change later.

Invite the children to help you make up some new versions of the rhyme. Start by substituting 'Sally' with the names of children in the group. Ask the children to try changing 'Saturday afternoon' to a different day of the week. Talk about what other things Sally might go round, such as the windy park or playground. Try out some of the children's suggestions to see if they fit the rhythm pattern. For example, the phrase 'the fish and chip shop down our road' doesn't fit, but 'the paddling pool' does.

Words on clay

Focus
Working with clay as a sensory stimulus for writing poetry.

What you need
A small lump of clay for each child in the group, a flip chart and marker pens.

Preparation
Give the children a lump of clay and let them play freely with it. Pick up and reinforce interesting words and actions used as they work the clay, for example 'It's all slippery', 'It's sticky on my hands' or 'Look, I'm making a snail shell.'

What to do
Hold a reminder session with the children to talk about what they did with the clay earlier. Tell them that together you are going to write a poem about having fun with clay.

Ask them to tell you how they used their hands to make different shapes and models. Jog their memories by saying things like 'I saw Rebecca rolling out a long, thin snake' or 'Winston, could you tell us how you made your holey pattern?' Can they describe how the clay felt in their hands as they rolled, squeezed or pressed it flat? Did it feel squidgy, slippery, cold, squirmy, sticky, oozy? What sort of words can they suggest to describe any sounds they noticed as they worked the clay? What did some of the end products look like? Write down the children's contributions as they suggest them.

When you have a bank of words from which to choose, ask the children to help you organise these into a poem. You could decide to have one verse about the actions they used (thump, press, squash), another describing what clay feels like and the last verse revealing what they made. They might like to use the phrase 'We've had fun in the clay today' as a chorus between each verse.

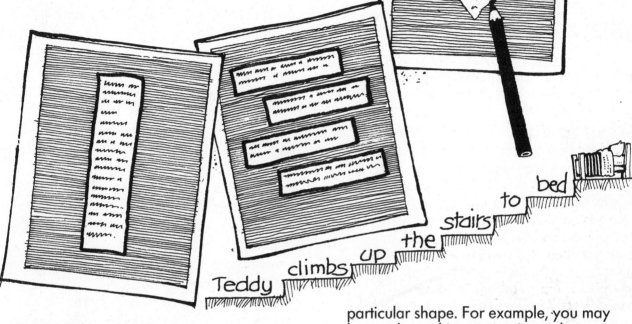

Get into shape

Focus
Helping to identify the special shapes of poems and rhymes.

What you need
Some poems with an obvious shape, clear-view folders, Chinagraph pencils or highlighter pens, pencils, paper.

Preparation
Read some of the poems to the children, tracking the words and lines to show the shape the poem makes on the page. Discuss how the words or lines are grouped so that they combine to make a particular shape. For example, you may have a long, thin poem using only two or three words on each line, or a poem written in a diamond or balloon shape.

What to do
Put some poems of different shapes into clear-view folders. Ask the children to draw round the outlines of these poems with a marker pen. Discuss the shapes they have traced.

Help the children to write some poems in a particular shape. The topic or theme you are working on with the children could provide a starting point. For example, words to describe your minibeasts could be written in a snail's spiral shape or as long wiggly worms. Others can be written in a staircase pattern as shown in the illustration.

Sounds fun

A Dibble-dubble Day

it's wet
dibble-dubble
it's wet
piddle-puddle
it's rained the
whole day long

the roof-top gutters
and the window shutters
splish-splosh
with the raindrops song –

'pitter-patter
potter-putter
split! splat! splot!

spitter-spatter
splotter-splutter
splish! splash! splosh!'

Joan Poulson

Focus
Having fun with the sounds suggested by words (onomatopoeia).

What you need
A poem which uses lots of onomatopoeia, such as 'A Dibble-dubble Day' by Joan Poulson in *Twinkle, Twinkle, Chocolate Bar* (OUP).

What to do
Read and enjoy the poem together, encouraging the children to join in with the rainy sound words. Read the poem again. Do the children recognise that the rainy sounds occur in the last two verses? Take one little phrase at a time such as 'pitter-patter', and use it to help evoke the sound of rain falling. Can they make it sound as if the raindrops are pounding on an umbrella? Try using the phrase to make the sound effects of a rain storm. Begin slowly and quietly, building up to a heavy, steady downpour. Gradually make the sounds die away until there is just a quiet and intermittent 'pitter-patter.'

Play with the beginning and end sounds. For example, *sssplat* or echoing the end sound in *splash*. Some children may recognise that they can alter words by simply changing the middle sound. For example, *splish, splash, splosh*. Make up some rainy day sounds of your own to say in turn round the class.

Follow-up
Try the same approach with machine sounds. Use body sounds (thigh slaps, foot stamps) and voice sounds (*whirrr, shshsh . . . phphpht*).

Lots of lovely lather

Focus
Working towards matching sounds and letters (alliteration).

What you need
Mrs Lather's Laundry by A. Ahlberg and A. Amstutz (Puffin); a few small objects, most, but not all, of which, begin with the letter *L*, a bag and a flip chart or chalkboard.

Preparation
Read the book with the children, giving them time to talk through the story and enjoy the humour.

What to do
Read the book again. Look at the title more closely. Point out (if they haven't noticed already) that the words 'Lather' and 'Laundry' begin with the same letter. Write the letter *L* in both upper and lower case on the board or flip chart. Is there anybody in the class (or other people known to the children) whose name begins with *L*? Enjoy fitting these names into the title to make new, alliterative ones of your own – 'Mr Lenny's Laundry' (Lara, Leone, Mrs Lopez and so on).

Play an alliteration game with your bag of objects. Tell the children that Mrs Lather only washes things begining with *L*, and that in the bag there are some things she will wash and some she won't (see illustration). The children then take turns to pick out an object. They should show it to the rest of the group and ask all of them to name it. Put all the *L* objects together and practise saying 'Mrs Lather launders lemons, . . . lions, . . . lollipops, . . . leaves . . .'

Write these words for the children and use them as the basis for a long list of *L* words. Add the children's suggestions to the list. Draw some simple picture symbols to help the children remember the words.

Follow-up
Take the children's list of *L* words into the hall or another large space. Adapt the traditional game of 'The farmer's in his den' to sing and act out 'Mrs Lather's in her laundry'. Sing it to the original tune, substituting a 'wish wash, wish wash' refrain. Begin each verse with 'She launders . . .'. Use the list as a reminder to help 'Mrs Lather' choose what she wants to 'launder' next. Examples might include the laundering of laughing lions, long ladders or little ladybirds.

A load of nonsense!

Focus
Playing with nonsense words.

What you need
Some nonsense rhymes such as 'Higglety, Pigglety, pop' (Samuel Goodrich) or 'In an oak there lived an owl' (traditional) in *Poetry Corner* (BBC).

What to do
Nonsense words and rhymes always go down well with young children. Free from conventional meaning, nonsense is a fun way of focusing attention on words themselves. Pick out some nonsense phrases from the poems listed above, and encourage the children to roll these new sounds around on their tongues until they can say them easily. Try saying the words at various speeds and experimenting with different voices (quiet, angry, happy). Let the children enjoy holding some nonsense conversations with each other.

Show them how it is possible to make new nonsense words by simply changing the initial letter. For example, Spike Milligan's 'On the Ning Nang Nong' (in *A Load of Nonsense*, Penguin) could become the 'Ting Tang Tong'. Ask the children to suggest other initial letters to use (perhaps the first letter of their names) and write the new words for them. Practise saying your new words, emphasising the sound of the initial letter.

Try putting one or two of these nonsense phrases together. Help the children to select their favourite combinations to say or sing together.

I've got rhythm

Focus
Enjoying poems with strong rhythms.

What you need
A poem with a strong, simple rhythm, evoking a train or machine such as David McCord's 'Song of the train' in *Noisy Poems* (OUP) or Clive Sansom's 'The train goes running along the line' in *Tiny Tim* (Picture Lions).

What to do
Teach the children David McCord's poem by asking them to echo each line after you. Emphasise the strong rhythmic pattern every time you say the poem together.

Introduce some simple body movements to help the children feel the rhythm. Try circular movements with arms at the side to represent the wheels turning, or rocking backwards and forwards. Use some words or phrases such as, 'clickety clack, clickety clackety, faster and faster', to tell the children a story about a train slowly pulling out of the station, gathering speed, zooming along, then slowing down again as it approaches its destination. Ask the children to act out your story by listening carefully to the phrases and matching up appropriate body movements. Can they speed up and slow down to match the speed of your voice?

Tap and guess

Focus
Recognising and playing the rhythm of familiar rhymes.

What you need
Six to ten strips of card long enough for you to write the first line of some nursery rhymes, a container to put them in, some simple pictures drawn or cut from magazines and stuck on to the appropriate cards to illustrate the rhymes, a wood block and beater.

What to do
Put the nursery rhyme cards into the box. Only include those which the children know very well and can say. Take out two cards and pin them up. Ensure that the children know what the words on the cards say. Encourage them to use the picture symbols as reminders. You could draw the rhythmic patterns underneath the words (see illustration).

Tell the children you are going to tap out (on the wood block) the rhythm of one of the nursery rhymes, and they then have to guess which one. Check their guesses by tapping out the rhythm again while they say the line very quietly to see if it matches. Select another two cards from the box and repeat this (see illustration). With practice, the children will be able to play the game with a partner. Provide a percussion instrument with the box of cards.

Tap and Guess

Humpty Dumpty sat on a wall

Little Bo Peep has lost her sheep

The long and the short

Focus
Listening to sound patterns in names; an introduction to syllables.

What you need
No special requirements.

Preparation
Use whatever opportunities you have to help the children familiarise themselves with the rhythms of their names — filling in the register or organising activity groups and so on. Clap and say names to make the children aware of names with long and short patterns.

What to do
When you are satisfied the children can say and clap their names in rhythmic patterns, choose three children to stand in a line so that you can clap their name rhythms in turn from left to right. Ask the children to listen while you do it first, then echo the pattern. Make sure the children have the rhythm of all three names firmly fixed in their minds.

Ask them to try changing the order (for instance, Nico swaps places with Miranda), and clap out the new sequence of names. Which patterns do the children like the sound of best? Try the same approach with other sets of three names.

Running around with rhyme

Focus
Developing the concept of rhyming words.

What you need
A large space, hoops, team bands.

Preparation

Immerse children in rhymes as often as you can. Say them over and over with the children so the concept of rhyme becomes familiar. Ask them to complete end rhymes such as, 'Mary, Mary, quite . . .' and 'Ding dong bell, Pussy's in the . . .'.

Play 'What's my rhyme?' Tell the children you are thinking, for example, of a little, furry animal that rhymes with house — can they guess what it is?

What to do

In a big space, divide the children into two teams called 'cats' and 'dogs'. Give each team different coloured bands. Lay out the hoops around the floor. The children must listen carefully as they run between the hoops while you say, for example, 'I'm thinking of an animal that rhymes with hat (fat, sat, pat, mat, splat and so on).' This is the signal for the cats only to jump into the hoops. 'Dogs' jump into the hoops when they hear the rhyme for their team (frog, log, Mog).

Moon and spoon

Focus

Beginning to match letter patterns to rhymes.

What you need

Copies of photocopiable pages 93 and 94, pieces of card; rhymes, poems and songs such as 'Polly had a dolly', 'I'm a little tea pot' and 'Bye Baby Bunting' which use the same letter patterns to make the rhyme, written up on poster-sized sheets of paper; a flip chart and marker pens.

Preparation

Tune the children into rhyming words by playing a quick game of rhyming 'I spy' or spot the odd one out. Read some of your selected rhymes to the children, pointing to the words as you say them.

Take a closer look at some of the rhyming lines. Can the children see that the two rhyming words are at the end? Circle the rhyming words in a different colour. Write some of these rhyming pairs on the flip chart or chalkboard. Write them under each other as a list so the children can focus on the letter patterns.

What to do

Cut out the 12 pictures on photocopiable pages 93 and 94 and stick them on to separate cards. Write the word on the back highlighting the rhyming patterns in a different colour. In pairs or a small group, give the children six cards (three pairs of rhyming words). First make sure they can find the matching pairs using the pictures only (for example, bell and shell). Shuffle the cards word side up. Can the children find matching pairs of letter patterns, such as dog and frog or hat and cat? When they think they have identified a matching pair, they can turn the card over to see the pictures. Ask them to say the rhyming pair aloud as a check.

Knock, knock . . .

Focus

Recognising and enjoying the pattern and humour of jokes.

What you need

Writing and drawing equipment, a flip chart or chalkboard, different coloured marker pens.

What to do

Jokes are not only fun but also help to focus the children's attention on the writing pattern of jokes and the rhythm of words.

Ask the children to act out some of their favourite knock, knock jokes and write out these jokes for them. As you are writing, highlight the fact that to make the joke funny we have to take turns to talk (this is also the beginning of script writing). Use two different coloured pens to show who speaks which parts of the joke. For example, child A says, 'Knock, knock'. (Write this in blue.) Child B says, 'Who's there?' (Write this in green on the opposite page as shown in the illustration.) The joke can then be read and enjoyed as a script.

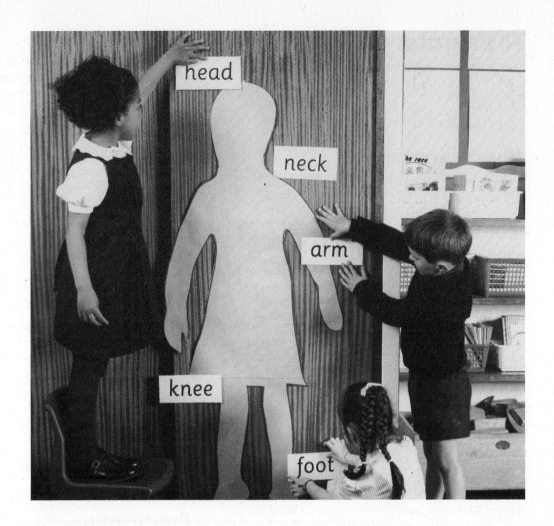

Writing across the curriculum

Chapter six

Children need to be able to write in many different ways in order to record all sorts of different information right across the curriculum. This chapter looks at how maths and science investigations, humanities, art and craft and music can give rise to a range of writing activities. Whatever you are doing, there will be opportunities to help the children see the need for, and use, different forms of writing.

Toys galore

Focus
Using classification to make a catalogue.

What you need
A selection of toys and games; toy, game and mail order catalogues, large sheets of paper, drawing and writing equipment.

Preparation
Show the children how a catalogue works. What is it for? How is it arranged? Help them to see that the toys and games have been grouped and shown as different sets (board games, soft toys and so on). Tell the children they are going to be making a toys and games catalogue of their own.

What to do
Start with a small selection of toys and games you have available such as soft toys, big toys, construction toys and jigsaw puzzles. Talk to the children about how they could put these into groups. Perhaps all the soft toys could go together, the wheeled toys could form another set and board games another. Use a set ring or separate sheets of paper for the children to practise different groupings.

Ask for the children's suggestions about which words would best sum up each of the sets. Write these set headings on separate pieces of paper, for example, 'Outside toys', 'Puzzles', 'Electronic games' as shown in the illustration. The catalogue can then be completed by listing toys under their appropriate headings. Start with those from your original collection, making sure the children understand which pages these belong to. The children could either draw and label their own pictures showing the

toys on offer, or find pictures in catalogues to cut out and stick on the correct page. Encourage them to use the catalogue in role play, where you could develop the idea of filling in order forms.

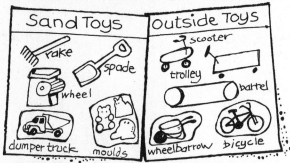

Mapping biscuits

Focus
The use of names and environmental print in a mapping diagram.

What you need
A collection of biscuit wrappers, a piece of card and a paper arrow for each child.

Preparation
Tell the children they are going to be finding out about favourite biscuits. Show them the wrappers and make sure they can distinguish the product name from the other writing on the packet.

What to do
Cut out the names of the biscuits and lay them in a column on the table. Tell the children to take turns to write their name on their card and place their arrow to indicate which biscuits they like best. Demonstrate this yourself first, to show the children that your name label shows who you are, the biscuit wrapper identifies the name of the biscuits to choose from, and the arrow shows which biscuit you like best as shown in the illustration.

Help the children to interpret the data. Discuss how many names point to each biscuit and make sure the children understand that this shows us which biscuits individuals preferred. Were there any biscuits nobody liked?

I've got a body

Focus
Making a labelled diagram showing parts of the body.

What you need
A sheet of paper large enough to draw round one of the children, small cards for labels, an action song such as 'I've got a body' from *Tinder-box* (A&C Black) or 'Head, shoulders, knees and toes' (traditional).

Preparation
Enjoy singing the song and practising the actions. This helps the children to link physical actions with the names of different parts of the body.

What to do
Make a picture list of all the different parts of the body mentioned in the song. Draw a nose, for example, and write the word next to it. Are there any other parts of the body the children can name and would like to add to the list? Read the list through together.

Draw round a child then cut round the outline and collage or paint your 'person'. Using the picture list to help them, ask the children to write their own labels to put on the body in the appropriate places. You could suggest they use an arrow to make sure the label is lined up in exactly the right position. Play a game of jumbling up the labels to see if the children can match them up again. The labelled picture could be displayed and used as a word bank for parts of the body as shown in the illustration.

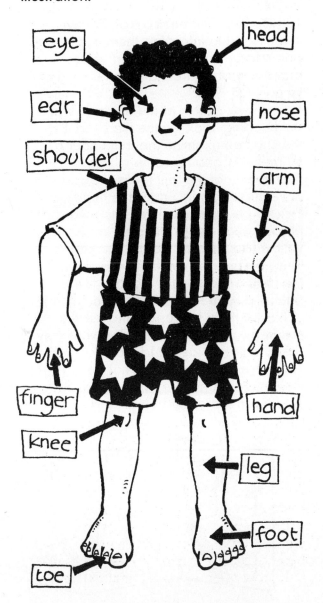

A sense of poetry

Focus
Writing a senses poem about fruit.

What you need
One type of fruit such as melon or kiwi, a knife, a flip chart and marker pens. Wash the fruit first and check that none of the children have allergic reactions before proceeding.

What to do
To help the children focus on the five senses, and to introduce them to a simple poem format, write five short verses together, concentrating on one sense at a time.

First look closely at the fruit and write the heading 'look' on the flip chart. Let the children examine the fruit under a magnifier. Consider some words to describe what the fruit looks like and write these as a list under the heading. Pick up on especially interesting words or phrases such as 'It's all hairy', or 'It's yellow like the sun'. Do the same for 'feel'. Before you cut the fruit open, ask the children to smell it. Do they like the smell – does it remind them of anything?

Now cut the fruit open and ask the children for words to describe what they see. Did they expect it to look like that? Are there lots of seeds? What patterns do they make? Are there any new smells? Add these words and phrases to your original lists. Write the heading 'taste' and invite the children to taste a piece of the fruit and describe how it feels in their mouths. Note down any sounds they heard as they bit into it – did it crunch or squeak?

Read through the words and phrases you have listed under each sense. Discuss which words the children would like to use for the final version. Do the same words appear more than once under each sense? Which ones sound good together? Would they like to change the order, or suggest other words? Write up the agreed wording on a large sheet of paper and enjoy reading the poem together.

Blob prints

Focus
Preparing a set of instructions for making a blob print.

What you need
Several sheets of paper, paint.

Preparation
Make some symmetrical blob prints with the children. As they are working, talk them through the order in which the process has to be done. Use words like 'First, we fold the paper in half. Next we put a blob of paint on the left-hand side . . . Last of all we open up the paper to show a butterfly.'

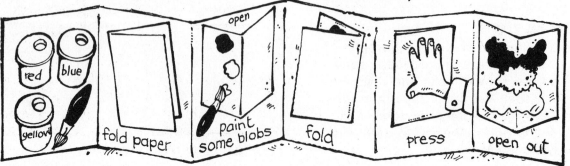

What to do

Tell the children that you may not always be there to show them how to make a blob print. How could they remember the sequence in which things have to be done — or show other people how to make one too?

Go through the blob print process again, focusing on how to leave clear, step-by-step instructions. As you talk through each stage, lay out the necessary equipment on the table top in the correct order. Set out the paint and paper first. Use another piece of paper to show that it needs to be folded in half. Put a blob of paint on one half of the next piece of paper and so on.

Talk through the process again, pointing to objects from left to right as you go, just as we read written material. Leave the materials out in sequence for other children to try. With some children you could go on to help them record their sequence in picture form on a concertina card. Encourage them to add labels such as 'fold', 'blobs of paint', 'open out' as shown in the illustration.

Teddy bears take the train

Focus

Using examples of environmental print (writing that we see around us everyday, such as signs) to help retell a story in sequence.

What you need

Teddy Bears Take the Train by S. Gretz and A. Sage (A&C Black), or any other picture book that shows examples of environmental signs.

Preparation

Read the book with the children and give them time to become familiar with the story and enjoy the illustrations.

What to do

Read the book again, encouraging the children to look carefully at the environmental writing used in the book. Ask questions such as 'Have you seen signs like this before?', 'Where do we see them?', 'What is the writing telling you?'

What information does the letter from the bears and Great-Uncle Jerome contain? Talk about the list the bears have written to help them remember what to pack. Look at the platform numbers and signs on the sides of the train carriages — what do the children think these are for? Look at what's on offer on the menu in the buffet car.

Go through the story again and this time make a picture list of some of the types of writing used (letter, list, ticket office, the engaged sign on the toilet door and so on). This will help the children to remember the sequence when they retell the story. Put some examples of these signs and forms of writing along with a copy of the book, into a small box for the children to use for retelling the story. The signs will act as 'sequence clues'. You might like to add a soft toy or play people as additional props.

Same story, different words

Focus
Adults and children writing about an event they have all been to.

What you need
Some adults willing to write; a school event such as a summer fayre, concert or assembly presentation; paper and pencils.

Preparation
Share your experiences of the event you have chosen to focus on. Talk about what you enjoyed most about it. Tell the children you would like to make a book about your special event, asking other people to write their thoughts and impressions.

What to do
As you sit with a group of children, begin by writing your contribution. Make sure they can all see what you are doing. In this way you will be providing them with a model for their own writing. Warm to your subject in order to let the children see that you are enjoying writing down your thoughts to share with others.

Encourage the children to share in and help you with your thought processes. Say things like 'What really stuck in my mind was . . .' and 'It was a sunny day . . . no, it wasn't just sunny, it was perfect weather for a summer fayre.' Show the children how you sometimes make mistakes at this stage of the writing process, change your mind or suddenly remember something really amusing you decide you just have to put in.

Ask the children to help you spell some of the words — what letter does each word begin with? Demonstrate that sometimes you don't want to stop and look for the word straight away; leave a space or draw a quick picture symbol and explain that you can always check it later. Respond to comments and questions such as 'Why did you do that?' or 'I know how to spell that word.'

Who else would the children like to ask to write a contribution in their book — parents, the vicar, friends? Invite some of these people in to write their version of the event with the children. You could make a fair copy and compile all the different versions into a big book to read and enjoy together. Make sure the children have understood that although everyone's words are different, they are all writing about the same subject.

Road names

Focus
Familiarising children with street names.

What you need
An opened box or large sheet of paper to make the 'play mat', small pieces of card for road name labels, the children's home addresses written out.

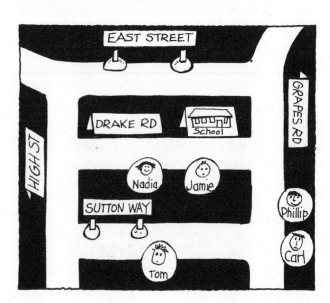

MR. D. Bear
Homeley Cottage
Porridge Lane
Oak Tree Wood
Bearhampton.

Preparation

Take the children out into the vicinity around the school to look at road names. Talk about what these signs mean — do any of the children live in these roads? What reasons can the children think of for having road signs? Who do they help (postman, visitors)? Look at where the signs are placed. Notice that some of the names use the word 'Lane', others use 'Road', 'Avenue' or 'Street'.

What to do

When you come back into class, help the children to make a simple road play mat of the road system you have just been looking at. Add a few local street names in the right places on the mat. Talk the

children through the route you took on the walk, recapping on the names of the roads and in which directions you turned to get from one road to another.

Show the children their home addresses — can they spot their road names? The children might like to add a small picture of a face with a name to show who lives in any of the roads you've labelled on the play mat. Leave the play mat out for the children to make up stories about going home from school, visiting neighbours or going shopping.

Follow-up

Ask the children to bring something in from home with their address on it — a letter, postcards, junk mail. Display these alongside examples of other written material which use street names such as street maps, directories, a local guide or Yellow Pages.

Young composers

Focus
Looking at musical notation.

What you need
Some music books showing staves (try to use songs or nursery rhymes the children already know and enjoy), manuscript paper, pencils.

Preparation
Show the music books to the children and explain that the printed words tell us which words to sing, while the other marks on the stave tell us the tune to play. Both have been written — the author writes the words and the composer makes up the tune. Tell the children they are going to be composers too.

What to do
Show the children how to read the notes from left to right across the stave and from top to bottom down the page — just like the lines in a book. Ask them to look carefully at the particular shapes of the notes (hollow, black, with sticks and tails). Try following the patterns they make up and down the stave — while singing the song or playing the tune to give an idea of how the music works. Leave out some manuscript paper with the music books for the children to have a go at writing some music of their own. Show them that their marks mean something by asking somebody to play the children's compositions back to them (or play them yourself if you know how). Ask your friendly musician to write down the names of some of the children's notes on the manuscript paper, so they can play their own tunes on chime bars. Make sure the children write their names on their compositions.

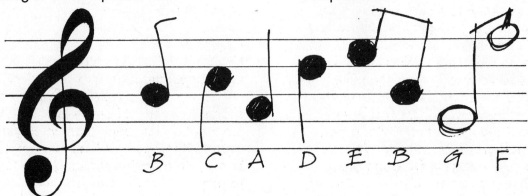

Draw and play

Focus
Writing down musical ideas for others to share.

What you need
A small selection of musical instruments (maracas, drum, tambourine, triangle, woodblock, guiro), drawing and writing materials.

What to do
Set up an area for children to play and experiment with the instruments freely at first. Then ask them to think about how to use the instruments to represent different parts of a story they know well, such as Goldilocks and the Three Bears. Which instruments could they use for Mummy, Daddy and Baby Bear? How should they play them — loudly or quietly, fast or slow? Encourage interesting rhythms and sequence patterns, such as a refrain for Goldilocks or a bang on the drum every time Daddy Bear comes in.

The children may enjoy sharing their compositions with others so they can play them too. Talk about ways of showing which instruments they used and in what order. How will other players know how many taps to play on each instrument and whether to play loudly or softly (see illustration)? Ask the children to draw picture symbols matching Daddy Bear with a drum, Mummy Bear with a woodblock and a triangle for Baby Bear, for example.

Follow-up
Use the instrument pictures on photocopiable page 95 for children to cut out and use to make more picture scores. Younger children could simply cut them out and arrange them in playing order. Others can add the number of beats with a symbol showing how loudly to play.

Shift that box

Focus
Developing language through drama.

What you need
A hall or large open space for the children to move around freely.

What to do
Pose some challenges for the children to act out. Try asking them to explore the difficulties of moving a really heavy box, for instance. Feel how big and heavy the pretend box is and pick up on any words or exclamations the children use. Ask them how they could possibly move such a big box. Which words could they use to describe how heavy it is or what happens to their bodies when they try to shift it?

Ask the children for other ideas for moving the box. Would ropes help to heave it along? Help them to see there are lots of different options such as sliding it, running it down a ramp, attaching wheels, using a skateboard, crane or a helpful elephant. Act out some of these suggestions, encouraging the children to describe and share with others what they are doing and how it feels. Try the same approach with other problem-solving scenarios, such as clambering up to pick apples from high branches or arranging the candles on a giant's birthday cake.

When you are back in the classroom, talk about what you have been doing and make a 'We can work it out book' to remind the children of some of their ingenious solutions, and to reinforce the describing words they used in the process.

Searching for words

Chapter seven

Beginner writers need strategies to help them find, build up and write words. In turn, these strategies will help the children to become independent writers. There are many different skills to master in the early stages. This chapter suggests activities to help familiarise the children with letter names, develop their visual awareness of letters and words, and support them as they begin to match letters to sounds.

Say and play

Focus
Using chime bars to familiarise children with letter names.

What you need
Chime bars A–G (add stickers if the letters are not clearly visible on the chime bars).

What to do
Introduce these activities to a group, then let the children try them independently. Play the chime bars in order from A to G. Tell the children that these notes have names. These letter names are also in the alphabet. Match them up to your alphabet frieze. Play the notes again and, with the children, say or sing the names of the notes.

Leave the children three chime bars to sing and play on their own. They should be placed in order from left to right to reinforce directionality in writing. After practice, change the three notes. The children can play them in alphabetical order or try other sequences, to help them learn letter names.

On the spot

Focus
Associating a letter name with a picture.

What you need
One of the gamesboards from photocopiable page 96 for each member of the group, 12 picture cards showing familiar objects (four each for the letters *b*, *s* and *m* – write the word on the back and highlight the initial letter, alternatively you can use any commercial game cards you have such as 'Lotto' or 'Snap'), counters.

What to do
Play the game with a small group. Give each child a copy of the sheet. Put the set of picture cards face up with the counters in the middle of the table. The idea is to cover the letter circles on the sheet with counters. Take turns to pick up a picture card and say the name of the letter that goes with that card, for example 'It's a *b* for ball.' Check that the correct letter has been identified by turning the card over before placing a counter on a *b* spot as shown in the illustration. If all the *b* spots are already covered, put the card back and wait until the next round.

Shopping for samosas

Focus
Associating initial letters with real objects in a play situation.

What you need
Your play house or a small area set up as a grocery shop, empty food packets, salt dough, separate cards for the letters *p* and *s*.

p pears
p pizza
p potatoes
p porridge
p poppadoms
s sausages
s sultanas
s samosa
s salt

Because the children will need to use the food words and their initial letters in their role play, it's a good idea to make a picture list with them. Draw a picture of some sausages, for example, and write the word next to it, highlighting the initial letter as shown in the illustration. Say the words with the children as you write them.

Leave some cards outside the shop with the letters *p* or *s* written on them. Before going into the shop, the children choose one of these cards and then ask the shopkeeper for some foods beginning with the letter they have in their hand. The shopkeeper uses the picture list to check that the goods requested do indeed begin with that letter. The customer is only allowed to put items beginning with that particular letter into the shopping basket. This approach can be adapted easily for other letters.

Letters in the limelight

Focus
Concentrating on the names, shapes and sounds of particular letters for a day.

What you need
Collage materials, a small collection of things beginning with a particular letter such as *t*.

Preparation
Tell the children you are going to have a special day finding out about the letter *t*. Ask them to bring things in from home beginning with *t*: teddies, a favourite T-shirt, perhaps a sentence or two written by parents, such as 'Thomas loves treacle tart for tea', or the name of another member of the family beginning with *T*.

Preparation
Tell the children you will be working together to set up a food shop for them to play in. Collect some empty food containers and help the children to make other foods from salt dough. Make sure you have four foods beginning with *s* (sausages, samosas, sultanas, salt, for example) and four beginning with *p* (pears, potatoes, pizza, porridge).

What to do

As the children are collecting and making items for the shop, ask them to make two separate sets, one for all the *p* foods and one for the *s* foods. Play a game of 'I spy' with the sets to focus the children's attention on the sounds of the initial letters.

What to do

Immerse the children in your chosen letter for the day, providing lots of different activities focusing on its various aspects.
● Set up a collection of *t* objects for the children to add to on the day. Play a game with them: choose two objects and make up some alliterative sentences to enjoy rolling the sound around on the tongue (two tiny teddies).
● Talk about the name of the letter. Do any of the children's names begin with *T*? Remind them that we always use a capital *T* for names. Try making sets of children with and without a *t* in their names.
● Make a collection of words beginning with capital *T* (book titles, countries, road names) and display them inside a big bubble outline of the letter 'T'.
● Make the letter *t* in lots of different ways: from pipe cleaners, adhesive and salt or sand, construction toys or nails as shown in the illustration.

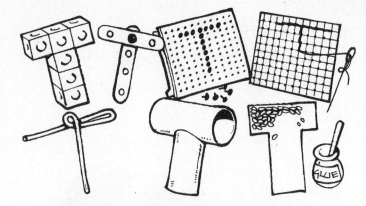

Alphabet

Focus

Getting to know the alphabet through sequence, letter names and sounds.

What you need

A collection of materials in which the content has been arranged alphabetically, such as an alphabet book and a picture index.

What to do

● Look at your own alphabet frieze, (or find an example in a picture dictionary or use a commercial alphabet strip). Explain to the children that the letters are always arranged in this order. Talk about the letter names and spot the letters used in their own names. Consider where Amy's name comes in the alphabet. Where would you look for Winston's name?
● Sing the alphabet to a familiar tune such as 'Twinkle, Twinkle, Little Star' to help the children learn the sequence.
● Look at some alphabet books with the children. Try Mog's *Amazing Birthday Caper* by J. Kerr (Collins), or *Lucy and Tom's ABC* by S. Hughes (Picture Puffin).
● Give the children four or five large plastic or wooden letters in sequence. Jumble them up — can they put them back in the correct order?
● Show the children the register so they can see how the alphabet has been used to order their names. Look at other materials which have been arranged in alphabetical order such as a card index, catalogues or an address book.
● Make your own large alphabet frieze of favourite foods. Use real packets or cut-out pictures to give the children the feel of different kinds of print and letter size.

Listen and run

Focus

Listening carefully to discriminate between sounds as a way into identifying sounds in words.

What you need

PE mats, a triangle, a tambourine and a tambour.

Preparation

Sensitise the children to listening carefully by playing a sounds game. Tell them you are going to play the tambour or the triangle. When they hear the tambour this is the signal to walk. The triangle means tiptoe quickly. Practise these sounds and movements one at a time, then change from one to another without warning. Introduce the tambourine and tell them this means skip. Can they change movements on cue?

What to do

In the hall or another suitable large open space, divide the children into two teams one called 'm' the other 's'. The teams each have a mat at either end of the hall as a team base. Call out words beginning with either of the team letters, saying something like 'I went to the shops and I bought a melon . . .'. Members of the 'm' team then run round the mats and back to their home base. The last back joins you to help decide which words to call out next. Keep going until the mats are empty.

Pat the cat

Focus

Building up words and recognising letter patterns.

What you need

Pat the Cat by C. and J. Hawkins (Picture Puffin); a piece of card with 'at' written on it, letter cards showing: *b, c, f, h, m, r, s* and *N, P, T*.

Preparation

Read the book to the children, giving them time to focus on the 'at' pattern and sound. Tell them they are going to be making their own class version of the book. Go through the book again identifying and discussing how the flaps work.

What you need

Show the children how, by adding a letter to the 'at' pattern, lots of different words can be made. Write down the list of 'at' words used in the book. Use word and letter cards to demonstrate how the word 'bat' is made by adding the letter *b* to the 'at' pattern; and 'mat' is 'at' with an *m* at the beginning and so on. Ask the children to say the words as you make them. Let the children make their own words with the letter and pattern cards.

Try making your own collection of 'at' sentences based on *Pat the Cat*. Give each child in the group a sheet of paper. Help them to make a sentence containing one 'at' word to illustrate, and write this on the paper. Write the initial letter on a card strip to pull down (as shown in the illustration).

Stuck for a word?

Focus
Talking about the word-finding strategies used in class.

What you need
A flip chart and marker pens, a poster-sized sheet of paper.

What to do
If children are to become independent writers they need to develop lots of different strategies for finding and writing words. The emphasis should be on children 'having a go' themselves, free from anxiety. Tell the children they will be helping you to make a poster to put up in the room to remind everyone of what they can do if they get stuck for a word.

On the flip chart, write down some ideas such as:
• leave a space (to show where the word should be);
• draw a picture (for the missing word);
• have a go (at any part of the word you can remember such as the first letter or the ending);
• search around the room (on name charts or on a display table).

Talk about where else the children could search for words before finally coming to you. These might include using an alphabet frieze, looking in your word banks or spotting the letter pattern on notice-boards.

Write up all the strategies you have discussed as a poster to display and use.

Sweet patterns

Focus
Spotting letter patterns on sweet wrappers.

What you need
A collection of sweet wrappers stuck on to separate pieces of card, (name side up), blank cards on which to write letter patterns.

Preparation
This activity helps children to create a visual image of some letter patterns needed for their own writing. Make sure they know the names of the sweets you have chosen. Prepare matching sets of letter pattern cards for each of the wrappers. For example, 'et' for *Secret*; 'is' for *Wispa*, 'ar' for *Smarties* and 'on' for *Lion* bar. Look carefully at the writing on the wrapper when you are choosing which ones to use. Make sure they match up to the letters you write on the cards. You may like to look later at cursive lettering and upper case letters.

What to do
With the children, look at the word *Lion* for example. How many letters make up the whole word? Talk about the names and shapes of the letters — match them up to your alphabet frieze or the children's names. Look at which letters are next to each other on the wrapper.

Give the children four wrappers and their corresponding letter patterns. Jumble up the letter pattern cards and ask the children to match each card to its wrapper.

Look, cover, write, check

Focus
Encouraging children to use a visual image to write their words.

What you need
A container for sand or a chalkboard.

What to do
Like other aspects of writing, spelling is best taught within the context of the children's own writing. Pick up on this to show the children how particular words are spelled. 'Look, cover, write, check' is a useful spelling strategy to develop.

Perhaps you are looking at the word 'as': ask the child to look carefully at the word. How many letters has it got? Write the word on a large piece of paper, talking through how you are forming the letters while the child watches. Now get them to trace around the letters with their forefinger to get a feel for the shape of the word. Say the letters together as the child traces them. Tell him or her to 'take a photograph' of the word in their mind to see the visual image as they close their eyes. Cover the word.

As soon as they have opened their eyes ask the child to reproduce the word in the damp sand (or use chalk and a board). Uncover the word and match it to their version — were they right? Praise them for any resemblance even if they haven't quite spelled it correctly. Have they used two letters? Were the letters right but written in the wrong order? Do they need to practise one of the letter shapes again? Encourage the children to try again — even if they got it right first time. Keep practising the 'look, cover, write, check' method to help fix the word in the visual memory. You might like to show the children how they can make new words with 'as' by simply adding a letter to the beginning or end: *has*, *was*, as*k*.

Danielle is building a tower

The action bank

Focus
Making a picture bank of action words.

What you need
Drawing and writing equipment.

Preparation
Explain to the children that they will be making a book of action words to help them in their writing activities. Focus on verbs by singing an action song or playing a game of 'Simon says' (walk, jump, fall down, leap like a frog and so on).

What to do
Working with a small group, remind the children of some of the things you have seen them do such as building a model, reading a book or digging in the sand. Talk about other things they enjoy doing and ask them to draw a picture of themselves doing one of these things. Get them to practise the action again before they draw. Encourage them to use lots of detail in their pictures by asking questions like 'Where were you when you were

building your model?', 'What did you use to make it?', 'How big was it?' Stress that the main thing you want to see is the action. Help the children to write a caption for their pictures so that whoever reads the book will be able to spot the action word easily. Help them to compose sentences such as 'This is Amarjit building a tower.' Highlight the doing words in a different coloured ink.

Compile the pictures and captions into a loose-leaf folder so that the children can add to them over time. Add to the collection any photographs you may have taken of the children doing various tasks indoors or on a visit. Ask them to bring in a picture of something they enjoy doing at home to add to the book. Read the book through with the children, emphasising the action words. Get them into the habit of referring to it during writing activities.

Banking on words

Focus
Helping the children to access a word bank.

What you need
Some examples of commercial word banks such as Usborne's *First 100 words* and *First 1000 words* series or *Words and pictures* by G. Edgar and G. McDonald (Child's Play); card and drawing materials.

What to do
With a small group, play a game to help them learn how to use a word bank. Take two word bank pictures such as a garden or hospital (or any others which relate to your current topic) and make some picture cards to match the words around each of the two picture-word banks. Select a small number of these cards and ask the children to find the matching words on the word bank (see illustration). Talk about where they should look for 'wheel barrow', for example. Is it more likely to be in the hospital picture or the garden?

Try making your own picture-word banks to complement your various topic activities.

Writing real books

Chapter eight

It is important to award the children's own writing the same status as the professional writers whose stories and poems you read together. There is also the need for children to understand how books work, so that they can try out various conventions and formats for themselves.

Books come in all shapes and sizes — lift-the-flap, peep-hole, zigzag, no text and so on. Display a range of these different sorts of books to give the children ideas and models for their own. Make sure the children's finished books are displayed alongside commercial ones for others to share and enjoy.

What's an author, Miss?

Focus
Helping the children to recognise what an author is, and that they are authors themselves.

What you need
No special requirements.

What to do
Gather the children together during 'carpet time' to look closely at a particular book. Help them to pick out the name of the author. Invite them to ask questions about what the author actually does. Do the children understand that the author is the person who wrote the words (and may also have drawn the illustrations), as opposed to actually producing the finished product? Do they know any other books written by the same author? Are there any biographical details about the writer on the book to help us establish that this is indeed a real person?

These are ideal opportunities to help the children really feel that they are authors too. Draw on some of their written examples to emphasise this point. Encourage the children to write their names on their own books so that others will know who the author is. Make sure the children's written work is displayed prominently alongside the other real books in your room.

Books in production

Focus
Setting up an area for the children to make their own books.

What you need
Commercial examples of different format books (pop-up, flap, rag, spiral-bound, big read-together books, peep-hole, miniature, boxed sets, concertina), a range of paper and card in different qualities, paper with borders, slide binders, sewing equipment, plastic pockets, a hole punch.

Preparation
Look at your range of books and talk to the children about how they have been put together. Let the children handle the books and enjoy discovering what happens when they pull the tabs or look through the peep holes. Focus on the connection between the shape of the book and its contents. Did they notice, for example, that in Eric Carle's book *Very Hungry Caterpillar* (Picture Puffin) the holes were made by the caterpillar eating?

What to do
Make sure the children have ready access to these different sorts of books to give them a model for their own book making. It helps to provide some home-made blank versions such as simple zigzag books and some pop-up shapes to start them off. Help the children to

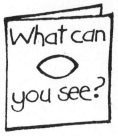
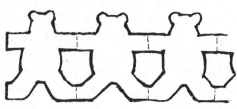

decide how many pages they want in their books. Discuss various ways of fixing the pages together: paper fasteners, stitching or putting the pages into a plastic pocket. When the children are creating stories of their own, remind them that they could use a special shape to make their book even more inviting. For example, if they are writing about a picnic in the countryside they could make a wavy line contour book to represent hills.

Lift the flap

Focus
Making a flap book and introducing the children to the question mark.

What you need
An example of a flap book such as *Where's Spot?* by Eric Hill (Heinemann) a flip chart or chalkboard, word cards, a sentence stand.

What to do
Explore the flap book with the children, giving them time to enjoy finding out how it works. Have they understood how the flap relates to the questions asked in the text? Read the book again and make a game of predicting which animal will be revealed under the flaps. Identify and talk about the question mark which appears after each question. Can they trace this shape in the air with their forefingers?

Help the children to write a 'sequel' to *Where's Spot?* Where else could Spot be hiding? Write the children's ideas down and show them how to put these into the form of questions. Use word cards and a sentence stand to make up questions together. Let the children place the question mark at the end of the sentence as they ask, for example, 'Is he in the garage?'

Choice story

Focus
Developing a story-line with the children and choosing endings.

What you need
A flip chart and coloured pens, paper, pencils and crayons.

What to do
You are going to be writing a story with the children to make an 'alternative endings' book for everyone to share. Start the story rolling by writing an opening such as 'Once, long ago, there lived a tall, thin wizard called . . .' Ask the children to suggest some good names for a wizard and write all these on the flip chart. Point out that now a decision has to be made. When you have agreed on the best name, circle your choice in a different colour and turn the page over.

Discuss a setting for the wizard's story and write down the children's ideas. For example, page two of your flip chart could say 'Now this wizard lived in a . . . cave/tree/castle.' Circle your choice again. Start each new aspect of the story on a new page. Help the children to make decisions about where the wizard went, who he met and how long the story is going to be.

Stop at an exciting point in your story and leave the final page of the flip chart blank. Tell the children you want them to decide how the story should end. Ask them to draw or write their own ending. You could scribe for the younger or less confident writers, helping them to see the need to write in a way which others will be able to read in the book later.

Follow-up

Write out the final version, using only your agreed highlighted choices, so the children can see the story as a whole. They may like to illustrate these sentences. Compile the children's suggested endings as the final page of a 'choice' story.

More than just words

Focus

Looking at illustrations as an important aspect of real books.

What you need

A selection of picture books showing a range of illustration techniques: collage, pastel, black and white line, and so on.

What to do

Share and enjoy your selection of books with the children. Help them make the distinction between the words and pictures by asking them to spot the red balloon or the little mouse in specific pictures. Ask questions like 'How many pictures are on this page?', 'Where is the writing on this page — is it at the top, under the picture or in a speech bubble as part of the picture?' Discuss the various types of illustrations used in the books: photographs, drawings, paintings, collage and so on. What colours has the illustrator used? Do the children like particular sorts of illustrations more than others?

Follow-up

Choose a book and look at the particular art techniques used in the illustrations. You might like to try Ezra Keats for collage, Brian Wildsmith and Eric Carle for finger-painting, comb scraping and spatter prints, or *Up and up* by Shirley Hughes (Red Fox) for black ink on cream paper. Invite the children to try out some of these techniques and use them to illustrate their own books.

Where next, Mr Bear?

Focus
Creating a sequel to a story book; highlighting locations and refrain.

What you need
Peace at Last by Jill Murphy (Macmillan), paper and pencils.

Preparation
Read the book with the children so that they become very familiar with the story, especially the refrain 'I can't stand this.' Invite them to join in with the refrain only while you read the rest.

Show the children how the words of Mr Bear's weary refrain can be arranged on a sentence stand. Talk about each of the words in turn, noting any letters which appear in the children's own names or other words with the same letter patterns they may know. As they become more proficient, the children can select and order these words on their own sentence stands, or try writing for themselves.

What to do
As you go through the story again, tell the children you would like them to suggest some other locations for Mr Bear to try. How can we remember where he has been already? The children could contribute to a picture list as you recall: the dripping tap in the kitchen, the ticking clock in the living room, the hedgehog snuffling in the garden and so on. Where else might he go? Add the children's ideas to the picture list.

After this initial brainstorm, give each of the children a sheet of paper for them to draw their suggestions for new locations and sources of irritating noises. Add a bubble to describe the sounds, for example 'Squeak, squeak went the swing in the park.' Then together make the 'I can't stand this,' refrain to add to the picture as shown in the illustration. Compile the children's contributions as a sequel to display alongside the original book.

Up front

Focus
A closer look at what makes up a front cover.

What you need
A selection of stories, some well-known and some new to the children; some non-fiction books.

What to do
With the children look at the front covers of some of the books you have selected. Help them to identify the major components of a front cover: title, author (illustrator) and usually a picture. Establish that the author is the person who wrote the words. Talk about how one author could have written lots of different books.

What clues can the children pick up from the title? Does it use the name of one of the story characters, or include part of a refrain or phrase used in the story, such as 'Peace at last'? Can the children predict what some stories might be about from the title?

Look more closely at the cover picture. Does it give any hints about the story setting or characters — might we be about to visit a farm or take a trip in space? Can the children speculate about the sorts of feelings and atmosphere the story might evoke? For example, does it look like a funny, mysterious or useful book? Do the children recognise any of the characters on the cover from favourite series such as Meg and Mog or Gretz's Bears?

Follow-up

Use these ideas to help the children plan their own front covers. Stress the importance of putting their names on the cover (as authors), and the link between the cover picture and the contents. Can the children suggest alternative titles for books they know well?

Writing with IT

Focus

Using a computer to help make a book and helping the children to make the link between words which are spoken and words which are written down.

What you need

A computer program such as *Fairy Tales* or *Old MacDonald's Farm* (BBC).

What to do

With a small group, make up a story from some of the picture options offered on the program. Talk about which characters the children would like to include, the sorts of places they might go and what might happen. When you have made up a story orally, using the pictures as a 'storyboard', suggest to the children that you could write their story down for them.

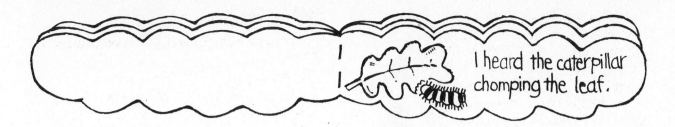

I heard the caterpillar chomping the leaf.

Key in the children's ideas, typing in exactly what they say. Read back the words from the screen. Scribing for them in this way means they will be more free to concentrate on the content rather than the technicalities of writing. Establish that the children have made the link between their spoken words and the words on the screen.

You could print out a copy of the story just as it is written, to give each child in the group a copy which looks professional. These can then be illustrated and shared with family and friends.

You may decide to take their writing a stage further by helping the children to edit their stories before printing out a final draft. Read the story with the group again, stopping from time to time to ask 'Is that what you really meant to say, or do you want to change anything?', 'What other words could you use instead of "said"?' Demonstrate how easy it is with a computer to change the order of things, make corrections or add more interesting describing words.

Caterpillar contours

Focus
Making an information book.

What you need
Some caterpillars or other minibeasts, a cut-out outline shape of your particular creature for each child in the group, non-fiction books about your minibeast.

What to do
As part of your minibeast topic, tell the children you would like them to make a book so other children can share what they have found out. Give the children plenty of opportunity during the day to observe the minibeast closely. Talk about what it looks and feels like, how it moves, what it eats and so on.

Remind them of some of the observations you have talked through during the day, then ask each child to draw or write one observation on the caterpillar shapes. They should talk it through first so that you can help them see how what we say sometimes changes when written down. Help the children to see that it is important to record their observations clearly so that other people who want to use the book can understand the written information easily. For example, a child might say 'It's nearly green like grass.' After discussion, this could be written 'The caterpillar is so green it could hide in the grass.'

Put these individual observations together as a class reference book to be displayed with other non-fiction books for everyone to use.

Bubble books

Focus
Looking at speech bubbles and how they are used in books.

What you need
Books showing speech bubbles such as *Meg on the Moon* H. Nicoll and J. Pienkowski (Picture Puffin) or *Snap! Snap!* C. and J. Hawkins (Armada Books), a flip chart and marker pen.

Preparation
At story times, read some books containing speech bubbles to the children. As you are reading, point to the words in the bubbles, pause, then emphasise the spoken sounds or words using appropriate voices.

What to do
The next time you read a 'bubble book' encourage the children to consider how we know which words are actually spoken in stories. How are these words shown? To help the children identify which words belong inside the speech bubbles, play a game where you read the narrative and the children join in with the words in the speech bubbles only.

Look again at the story and discuss what else Meg (or any other character) may have said. Use the flip chart to demonstrate how the children's suggestions can be shown in speech bubbles. An example might be: 'Meg said, "What a lot of rubbish," as they landed on the moon.'

Follow-up
Make your own big Meg and Mog story book. Give the children a paper cut-out speech bubble and ask them to draw a picture of one part of the story (or a specific event). Help them to write inside the speech bubble what they think the character might be saying. The bubbles can then be changed around to put different words into the mouths of Meg, Mog and Owl (see illustration).

Library land

Focus
Understanding that books have been written for other people to enjoy; children are authors too.

What you need
A play house or play area, drawing and writing materials, some library membership forms, a small collection of books.

Preparation
Take the children on a visit to your school or local library to give them a feel of how it works and to show them that libraries are quiet, cosy places where we can go to read. Show them how the books are arranged to make them easier to find.

What to do
Involve the children in planning how to turn your role play area into a library. Can they recall and discuss some of the things they noticed during your visit? Consider what useful things they will need to help keep track of all the books: tickets, cards, a date stamp, reminder slips and so on.

Ask the children for their ideas about how the books might be arranged so that people can find them easily. Would it be a good idea to separate fiction from non-fiction? Would they like to 'theme' the books under categories such as animals, homes, transport and so on? Would it be nice to have a beanbag or armchair to sit on and some newspapers to read?

Let the children play freely in their new library environment. You could set challenges occasionally. For example, ask 'How could you encourage more people to come into your library — how about featuring an author of the week?' or 'How will you be able to remember which books people have ordered specially?'

Follow-up
● Foster the feeling of children being real authors by providing a special shelf in the library to display books they have written themselves.
● Have story-telling and 'meet the author' sessions where the children share their own books with the rest of the group. Draw on the opportunities provided by 'National Book Week' for children to write and share real books with professional authors.

WE CAN WRITE AT HOME

You may have written something at home this week
* Look at the list with your child
* Put a ✓ or ✗ in the boxes

a note to the milkman ⬚

a greetings card ⬚

a phone message ⬚

a shopping list ⬚

a postcard or letter ⬚

a video label ⬚

a gift tag ⬚

an order form ⬚

a crossword or puzzle ⬚

*Anything else [＿＿＿＿＿＿＿＿＿]

* Have you any writing your child could bring to school please?

Write this way, see page 28

Get in sequence, see page 31

To
_____

Please come to a party

On _____

At _____

Love from _____

CUT ✂

R.S.V.P Thank you. I can come to your party   Love from
         I'm sorry. I can't come to your party   _____

to _____

You are invited to a party

On _____

At _____

Love from _____

✂

R.S.V.P Thank you. I can come to your party.   Love from
         I'm sorry. I can't come to your party.   _____

Moon and spoon, see page 59

Moon and spoon, see page 59

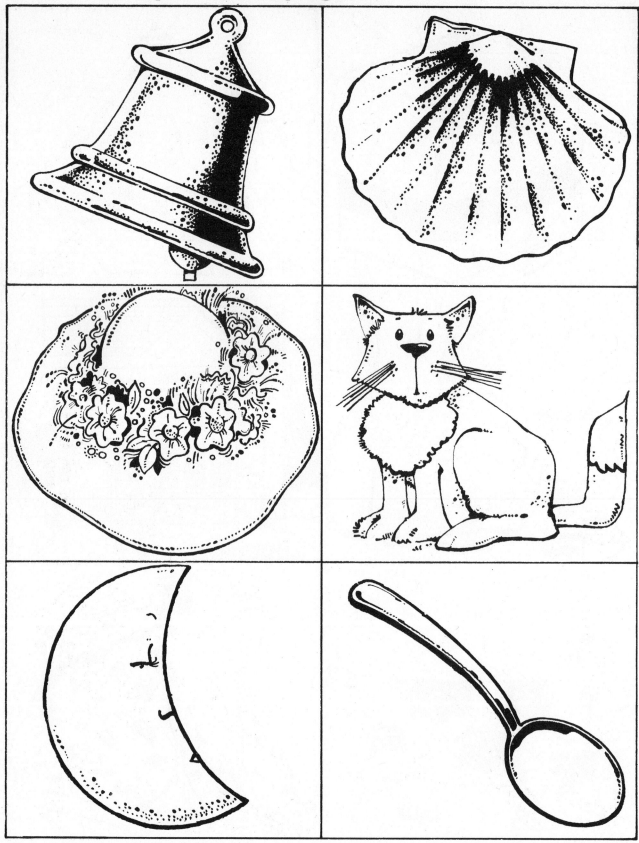

Draw and play, see page 69

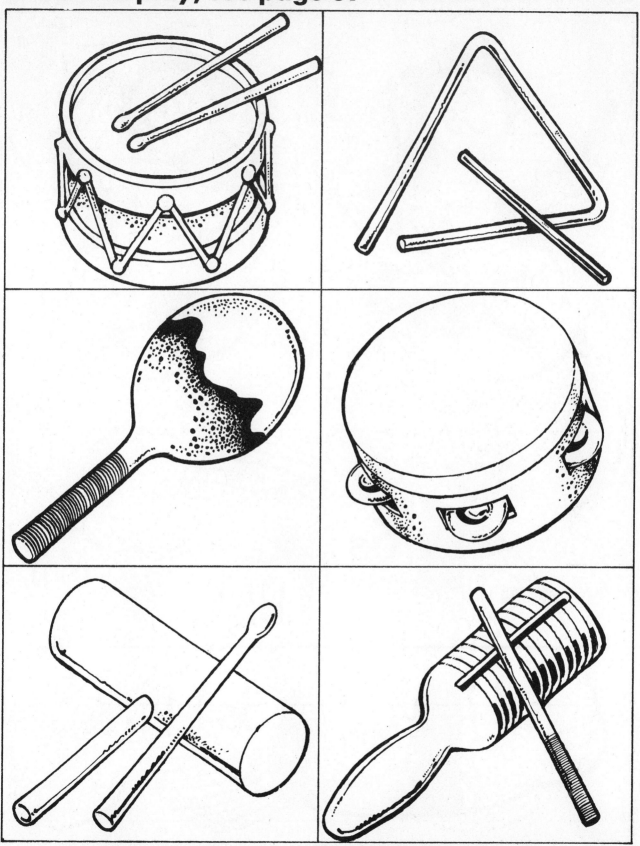

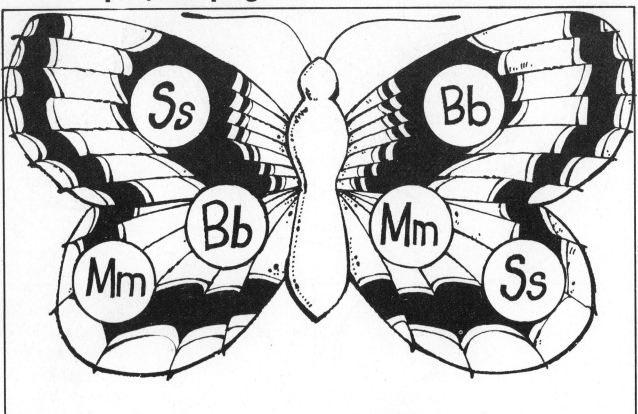

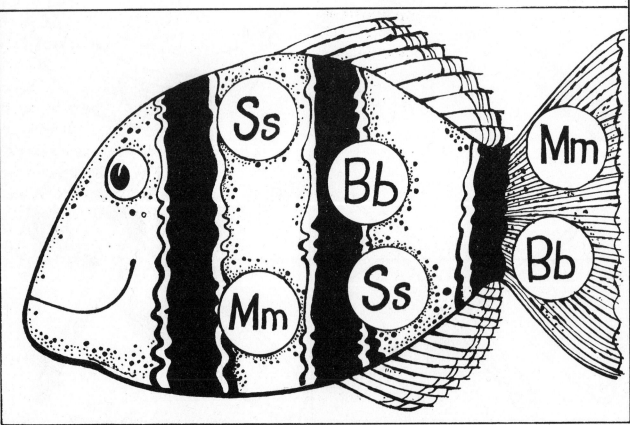